THE BLOOMSBURY GUIDE TO

CREATING
ILLUSTRATED
CHILDREN'S BOOKS

THE BLOOMSBURY GUIDE TO
CREATING ILLUSTRATED CHILDREN'S BOOKS

DESDEMONA McCANNON
SUE THORNTON
AND
YADZIA WILLIAMS

A QUARTO BOOK

Published in 2008 by
A&C Black Publishers
38 Soho Square
London W1D 3HB
www.acblack.com

ISBN: 978-1-4081-0574-0

Conceived, designed and produced by
Quarto Publishing plc
The Old Brewery
6 Blundell Street
London N7 9BH

QUA: ECI

Editor: Liz Dalby
Indexer: Diana LeCore
Art director: Caroline Guest
Art editor: Emma Clayton
Designers: Joelle Wheelwright,
Karin Skanberg, Tania Field,
Jess Wilson
Picture research: Sarah Bell
Editorial assistant: Amy Kopecky
Photographer: Martin Norris,

Creative director: Moira Clinch
Publisher: Paul Carslake

Colour separation by
Modern Age Repro House Ltd, Hong Kong
Printed by SNP Leefung Printers Ltd, China

9 8 7 6 5 4 3 2 1

CONTENTS

INTRODUCTION

Picture books invite children into imaginary worlds, introducing them to the idea of written language and its relationship to the real world. At their best they engage and entertain, instilling children with a love of books and an inquisitive mode of reading that will last their whole lives.

CRASH COURSE

The Children's Writers' and Artists' Yearbook
Published annually, this almanac provides you with vital information about how to protect your copyright, how to send out your work and lists up-to-date contacts and addresses.

METHODS OF ENGAGEMENT

Children love to be read to, but they also like the independence and flexibility of reading a book for themselves. Both experiences are valuable. If read to they can listen to the narrative and look at the pictures simultaneously. If reading alone they can actively engage their imagination and construct the story for themselves.

FIT FOR PURPOSE

Picture books give adults and children common ground – to start a conversation about something in the book, to clarify words that the child does not understand or to share a joke contained in the text or pictures. Most importantly, a book creates a "safe zone" of nurture and understanding between the reader, the child audience and the imaginative world they are both sharing. The best books leave a positive lasting impression and evoke a safe atmosphere for the child's development. But be advised that not all children's books are beneficial. If a book is unsatisfying, cynical or plays upon clichéd scenarios, the chances are the author only cared about his next sell.

Arthur Burdett Frost
Arthur Burdett Frost was born in Philadelphia in 1851. He was famous for his illustrations of animals and people, notably Brer Rabbit.

Charles Henry Bennett
Charles Henry Bennett was an untrained comic illustrator who illustrated several books, including *The Fables of Aesop*.

The world of children's book publishing is driven by many factors – a good story, beautiful illustrations and educational benefit all play a part in the decision to develop a book. The overriding concern of publishers, however, is that the book should succeed in the marketplace.

WHO BUYS CHILDREN'S BOOKS?

Adults buy books for children for a variety of reasons. Educators and librarians have specific remits and requirements; they will be guided by a curriculum to teach and the budget they have to spend. Aunties and grandparents looking for a birthday present often want to buy a special book that will be cherished in years to come. Harassed parents in the supermarket may simply want something that will distract and entertain. A parent and child may take a special trip to the bookshop to pick out a story for bedtime reading, and this can be a treat for both the adult and child.

Publishers of children's books are aware of the different markets that they sell books into and have marketing departments devoted to monitoring and evaluating the financial success of their books. It will probably help you to have an understanding of these commercial demands when you are pitching your picture book idea. Knowing your audience, and also knowing where your idea "fits into" the market, will help give you a stronger case for the publication of your book.

CRASH COURSE

The Uses of Enchantment
by Bruno Bettelheim
(1976)

This is a key text in understanding how fairy stories aid a child's psychological development.

Spells of Enchantment: The Wondrous Fairy Tales of Western Culture
by Jack Zipes (1992)

A collection of literary fairy tales, showing how the story concerns and structures have changed over time.

Collections of fairy tales:

- The Brothers Grimm
- Hans Christian Andersen
- Mother Goose

Fairy tales never get stale. Read some of the stories above and try writing a fairy tale of your own.

A GLOBAL INDUSTRY

The children's picture-book industry is a global concern. Publishers are usually keen to create co-editions with international publishers to maximize profits and lower the cost of producing each individual book. Each year publishers gather at the Bologna Children's Book Fair in Italy to do business with each other and keep up-to-date with global trends in children's books. If you are interested in becoming a children's book author it would be worth trying to attend an international event like this. Visit the bookfair's website at www.bookfair.bolognafiere.it

Bologna Children's Book Fair
The Bologna Children's Book Fair is a huge international event attended by book publishers and others involved in the industry. It can be a rich source of ideas and information on what's "hot" in the children's book world.

THINK OF YOUR MARKET
A cute little character, highly appealing for a
"picture book" readership (see page 12).

Chapter one

CREATING CHILDREN'S BOOKS

An introduction to the subject of children's books – from the importance of understanding your target market to a general look at possible subjects and themes – this section will help you develop a methodology for brainstorming and researching ideas.

1

THE IDEA OF A PICTURE BOOK

A picture book provides an opportunity for a child and an adult to enjoy sharing something together. It is an event as well as an artefact. The "idea of the book" resides in the people who experience it, and the experience of the book is not as straightforward as you may imagine.

A picture book may seem to be a simple proposition – a decorated story. In fact, a picture book contains several modes of expression and can contain multiple layers of meaning. What a picture book "means" to a child is more than just a story with illustrations. From an early age, children learn what a book is, how to hold it the right way up, the order in which to turn the pages and how to read – first the images and then later the words. The imagery may be "realistic" or entirely graphic. Imagery and colours may form patterns throughout the book, accruing meaning as motif; white space may imply content and demand that the child mentally "fill in the gaps"; and the illustrations may expand on and extend the information in the text. Sometimes, the illustrations may even tell a different story. This tension between what is said and what is shown makes picture books a unique and exciting form of graphic expression.

Struwwelpeter

Writer and illustrator Maurice Sendak rates *Struwwelpeter* by Heinrich Hoffmann as one of the most beautiful picture books ever made. It is interesting to see such early examples of the picture book form (*Struwwelpeter* was first published in 1845) and compare them with what we think of as innovative design today. The use of white space, typography and borders to create the landscape of each morality tale is very "modern" in the way it creates an imaginary world and draws attention to the surface of the book.

TRY THIS

It is worth looking carefully at how picture books work before you embark on one of your own. Take an example that you like and analyze how the images and text work together. Study the visual language of the book. Make sketches of the layouts and ask yourself why they are successful. Is the typography graphically expressive? Does it help the child to understand the book, or could it interfere with the legibility? (Does this matter?) Is the book appropriate for its audience? What makes you assume this?

An interesting exercise is to create a story about a child with an imaginary friend that only they can see. Consider how the illustrations will convey the disparity between the child's perception of reality and what is actually there. *Not a Box* by Antoinette Portis (HarperCollins, 2006) is a great example of this.

BEYOND WORDS AND PICTURES

Illustrations may "interrogate" the text by adding to or saying less than the words next to them, but equally important to the deeper message of the book is its format, the stock it is printed on and even the smell of the ink. Consider books from your own childhood – the tactile qualities of them probably remain as part of the memory. When you plan a picture book in a holistic way, remember that the message of your book – its atmosphere – will not reside in the words and pictures alone, but in the complete experience of the book.

COMMUNICATING THE IDEA

When you start to develop an idea for a picture book, bear in mind that the book is a combination of words and pictures, and both are equally important in communicating the overall message and atmosphere. If you are not confident as a writer, or do not think you can draw well enough to illustrate your own story, you may consider collaborating with someone else. However, it is worth developing the book holistically, sketching out ideas alongside drafting the text, and making small dummy books (see page 138) to test whether the pacing of the story works. In some ways developing a picture book is analogous to working out a film sequence – there are similar concerns of angles of view, composition and cutting to significant key frames. Think of a picture book as a condensed, effectively edited storyboard.

Tactile imagery
Books can be interactive and convey information in many different ways.

Illustrating key moments
Illustrations should show the action of the story at key moments, and add to the drama and surprise of the narrative.

CRASH COURSE

Words about Pictures:
The Narrative Art of
Children's Picture Books
by Perry Nodelman (1988)
This book remains a key text in describing and unpacking the ways in which a picture book communicates with a child audience.

Alice's Adventures Underground
by Lewis Carroll
The first draft of the famous children's book *Alice in Wonderland* was heavily annotated with sketches for the illustrator Tenniel to work from. Charles Dodgson (Lewis Carroll) had very clear ideas about how the images should relate to the text.

2 TARGET MARKETS

Relating to your target audience – children – means learning to communicate using words and images that are recognizable and understandable to them. Children have a variety of different attention spans, anxieties and interests. It is difficult to generalize, although picture books do tend to be put into age-related categories (see below).

In a bid to create characters and stories with unique characteristics but universal appeal, the writer and illustrator will often rely on cliché and stereotypes. This can reflect more about the attitudes of those creating the books than the experiences of their readership. For example, the archetypal kindly grandma with grey hair, slippers and cardigan, clutching her knitting hardly reflects the dynamic and glamorous woman a child may know as his or her own grandmother.

Whether you choose to reinforce or challenge the prevalent attitudes towards age, gender, race or disability is up to you. Just remember that what you may find a convenient visual shorthand, someone else could interpret as offensive. Try to always keep in mind that the world of storybook norms is a fiercely strong influence on how a child will grow up thinking about themselves and those around them.

Subvert stereotypes
Maybe older ladies do wear tweed... but if they do, consider that maybe their pets do too.

CHILDREN'S AGES AND CORRESPONDING BOOKS

- **0 to 3 years:** board books, novelty books
- **3 to 5 years:** picture books, ABC books
- **5 to 7 years:** picture books, reading primers, colour storybooks
- **7 to 9 years:** black and white stories, novels, comics
- **9 to 11 years:** short stories, poetry, novels, graphic novels
- **11 years+:** "young adult" fiction

Some books challenge the preconceptions of age-related categories – for example, so-called "reluctant reader" books are written in simple language but are illustrated to appeal to an older age group.

CHILDREN'S TASTES

Every child is unique, although television, books, peer pressure and the attitudes of adults will all have an effect on their tastes. Although the publishing industry is dominated by a "pink is for girls, pirates are for boys" attitude, it is possible to create characters that appeal to both sexes.

Gender programming
Do you agree that girls love ballet and boys want to play cowboys? It is good to be aware of the values inherent in these stereotypes, and decide whether you would like to support or challenge them in your work.

FIRST EXPERIENCES

Consider your own childhood "firsts" – going to the dentist, school or hospital for the first time dealing with bullying coping with the death of a pet or a relative learning where babies come from and so on – and recollect any other significant childhood experiences. Many such events are serious issues for a child, and reading a story that enables them to talk about it or hear the perspective from someone else can be a great support and comfort.

OLDER CHILDREN

If you have the ability to draw older children, include black and white examples of illustrations of them in your portfolio; you may receive commissions for storybooks and non-fiction. There is also a market for the illustration of children's books for reluctant readers, with older characters but not text-heavy, in which comic-style storyboarding plays a more significant role.

Depicting roles
What do you think this woman's role in life might be: wife, mother, daughter, worker – or all of the above?

Tweed or sneakers?
In this illustration from *Vegetable Glue* by Susan Chandler and Elena Odriozola (Meadowside Children's Books, 2008), the frail grandmother stereotype is challenged by the depiction of a dynamic, healthy older woman who shows the value of eating your vegetables!

TRY THIS

Happy families

- Many picture books are conceived around the staple routines of family life, but do remember that the stereotypical four-person family often displayed in picture books is not the only sort of family that exists.

- Create a set of cards showing a family group. There should be at least one parent, a child and an older person in each set. They do not have to be "realistic" but should have a shared "culture", be it ethnic or metaphorical. For example they could be West Indian, superheroes or both!

- On the back of each card write a profile of the character, what his or her interests are, their personality and so on.

- Use this project to reflect on the way we depict different ages, genders and cultural groups, and our perception of roles within the family.

READ THIS

Girls, Boys, Books, Toys: Gender in Children's Literature and Culture
by Beverly Lyon Clark and Margaret R. Higonnet (2000)
This book provides an introduction from a feminist viewpoint to the issues and terminologies surrounding children's culture.

3 THEMES

Children's stories can be categorized into general themes. They often address experiences that are difficult for a child to understand in adult terms, such as the conflicting feelings aroused by the arrival of a new baby, the death of a family member or moving house.

ARCHETYPES AND RULES

A story can be based upon any aspect of experience – a daunting prospect for the aspiring writer, as the scope for content is infinite. Much has been written about the grammar of storytelling, and there are plenty of books that offer formulae and structural advice on how a story should progress. Jungian and archetypal literary criticism sees stories in terms of phases such as "the call to adventure", "the refusal of the call", "the threshold test" and so on. This can be helpful in analyzing what you have written, but do not feel bound by a set of rules. They can all be reduced to one maxim: "a story should have a beginning, a middle and an end". Do not be distracted from telling a story by overly didactic rules. If your idea has heart and the story has an authentic emotional core it will be more affecting and effective than formulaic rhetoric.

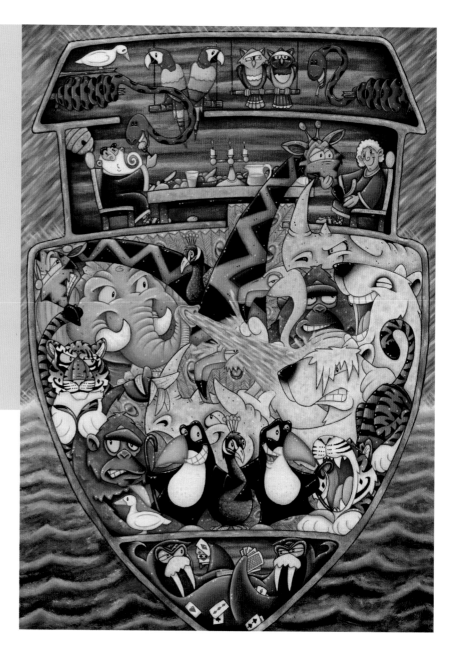

Cultural themes
Stories are passed down through generations and become part of our shared cultural identity. It is interesting to see how similar many of these stories are. How many different flood stories can you find, for example?

THE OLDEST STORIES

Some of the oldest stories, myths and legends emerged from the desire to explain internal psychological conflict in concrete terms. The names of characters, monsters and gods have become absorbed into our language and are now used to describe archetypal situations – for example "Oedipus complex", "Cupid and Pysche" or "Echo and Narcissus". Try reading some Greek myths and think about the themes and ideas within them that still resonate today.

Myths

Myths are the received wisdom of a culture expressed in symbolic and allegorical form. Often involving supernatural characters, they express archetypal human situations.

Metaphor

When a story is described as being "disguised", the use of metaphor is generally what is being referred to – understanding things in terms of other things. Aesop, whose fables are some of the oldest surviving stories, uses the characteristics of animals to express aspects of human behaviour and common moral dilemmas.

The Fox and the Stork

The story of *The Fox and the Stork* represents human behaviour metaphorically by substituting animals and presenting a dilemma in terms of a specific encounter. The fox cannot eat from a tall vase; the stork cannot lick from a plate. The story is about difference and pragmatic relationships, and is also quite entertaining!

TRY THIS

The Fables of Aesop

Find a collection of Aesop's fables (you can find them online) and list the clear moral themes suggested by each. You may decide that some have more than one. This is what makes storytelling fascinating – a complex or multi-faceted problem can be presented effectively in a very simple way.

CLASSIC CHILDREN'S STORY THEMES

- **Courage:** Adventure; overcoming fears; a hero who finds strength in himself where he thought he had none. *Hiccup: the Viking Who was Seasick* by Cressida Cowell (2001) is a good example of this.

- **Friendship:** Sharing and helping each other; resolving conflict; good times. *Best Friends for Frances* by Russell Hoban (2002) is an example of this theme.

- **Loss:** This common theme reflects a central anxiety among children. It can be something huge like the loss of a grandparent or something as everyday as the loss of a toy, but the underlying anxiety is the same. It can make for a simple pivotal plot too, when the thing that is lost is found at the end. A slightly offbeat example is *The Lost Thing* by Shaun Tan (2000).

- **Growing up:** Accepting change; not always getting what you want or having to wait for things; changing attitudes toward the opposite sex. This theme is about learning a

lesson from life that enables you to mature. *The Giving Tree* by Shel Silverstein (1964) is a book that encourages empathy.

- **Belonging:** Children are conformists and enjoy stories about belonging to a group – however, this needs to be shown sensitively. The related theme of "difference" also addresses anxiety about not fitting in and can be a helpful way of promoting tolerance and understanding. Rosemary Wells' *Yoko* books (2001) are good examples.

- **Anger:** An important theme, offering reassurance to children that they are not alone in their feelings, and ways of visualizing beyond the lack of control. Children have an acute sense of unfairness and are often aware of their lack of power in situations. *Angry Arthur* by Hiawyn Oram (1993) and *Where the Wild Things Are* by Maurice Sendak (1963) are both good examples.

- **Jealousy:** Related to the theme of anger, but more specific. There are many books that address the feelings aroused by the arrival of a new baby. *Ginger* by Charlotte Voake (1998) is an example of this theme being handled creatively.

- **Love:** Perhaps the biggest theme of all in children's books. Affirming your love for someone and being loved in return is the lynchpin of a happy childhood, and picture books offer both the occasion (being read to) and the means by which to share this. *Guess How Much I Love You* by Sam McBratney (1996) is a good example.

As you can see, this list centres around a nexus of anxieties and desires that a child experiences. There are many different ways that these can be disguised and acted out, but essentially all stories address a problem and offer strategies for its solution, however surreal and fantastical the protagonists and settings may be.

Resolving jealousy

In *Ginger*, by Charlotte Voake, Ginger the cat is upset by the arrival of a new kitten, but eventually accepts and befriends it. The theme is jealousy, and the problem is resolved with quiet humour by the interplay between the illustrations and the text.

TESTING YOUR IDEAS

Running workshops with children is fantastically rewarding, and the feedback you get can be hugely valuable to the development of a book idea. This can involve either going out into schools or bringing a group of schoolchildren into your learning environment to create imagery together and talk about what makes a book a success.

Activities for children
Harnessing the creativity of children through workshop activities can be a great way of finding out what they like and what they don't.

Case study 1

Students on the Illustration for Children's Publishing course at North East Wales Institute (NEWI) in the UK ran a workshop with pupils at a local school. The students' aim was to test the children's "visual literacy" in drawing concepts and information as characters, which the children then used as a basis for creating narratives. This research enabled the students to draw conclusions about how well children could decode conceptual information from imagery without any text. Children's visual literacy is highly developed but often underused in the school curriculum. This pilot project provided material that went on to form the basis of several more research projects and the students also found that it had implications for the way information could be presented to children.

Case study 2

A group of NEWI students also collaborated with children to create a "circus in a day", providing materials and sharing what they knew about circuses in order to create a short animation. The children then created a program for their own "super silly circus" and gave all the characters names. The benefits of collaborating with children in this way are enormous. You can use their spontaneous responses to gauge whether they are enthusiastic about a particular theme or idea that you introduce.

Case study 3

Some students ran workshops in schools in which they presented their work in progress on a story idea in development to a group of children. The children gave the students feedback on their artwork and story ideas. It is always useful to listen to the opinions of children, although in the end you must keep in mind that a few are not representative of all children. Their opinions may conflict with your own understanding of a book – consider carefully whether or not to act on them.

Practical advice

- You must ensure that you have had a criminal record check to reassure a host school or organization that the children will be safe with you.

- Make sure you carry out a "risk assessment" if you are setting up a workshop of your own.

- If you do arrange to visit a school, try to arrange to work alongside experienced teachers if you have no experience of working with children.

4 COMING UP WITH AN IDEA

A blank sheet of paper can be a terrifying prospect and, although you may feel you have latent talent as a creator of children's picture books, it can be hard to start. The following practical suggestions may help.

Character ideas
Working through character ideas in a sketchbook is a good place to start. Imagine the characters engaged in different activities.

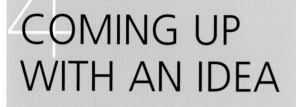

you develop the "antennae" to gauge whether your own creations will appeal to a child.

WRITE FOR A PARTICULAR CHILD

It is impossible to write for the generic idea of "children", and if you have children of your own or regularly encounter them you will know that this is true. That is the reason why so many successful children's books have been written for a particular child. For example, Charles Dodgson (Lewis Carroll) wrote *Alice Underground* (the precursor to *Alice in Wonderland*) for his young friend Alice Liddell, and Kathleen Hale wrote the *Orlando* books for her own children.

BASE A CHARACTER ON A CHILD YOU KNOW

Base a character on a child that you know well and put them in a new situation. For example, *Little Lord Fauntleroy* was based on Frances Hodgson Burnett's own son. Even if the character you create takes another, non-human form, the child it is based upon will give it authenticity. Russell Hoban's badger character, Frances,

THINK ABOUT YOUR OWN CHILDHOOD

List memories from your childhood, including your favourite foods, sweets, clothes, board games, toys, journeys, adults, holidays or particular incidents. This is a useful exercise because it reinforces the sense that all children are different in the way they respond to the world. Try to access the sensations of your particular childhood. There may be material for a story there, or it may help you create imagery with a unique atmosphere. Tapping into these memories will help is so acutely portrayed with her songs and sayings that it is hard to believe she is not based on a real little girl.

START WITH OBSERVATIONAL DRAWING

Visit your local zoo and spend time observing and drawing the animals, concentrating on one or two of them to really get a sense of their personality. Drawing from life, even if you feel that your observational drawing skills are not strong, will help focus your attention; you will notice much more detail, and it will be easier to recall back in the studio. This is also true of drawing in art galleries and museums or drawing landscapes, architecture and people in cafés and on trains. Take any opportunity that you can to draw.

START WITH A CHARACTER

Try creating a set of "Happy Families" cards (above), with information about each character written on the back. Base them on families you know, animals, robots, amoebas, superheroes, vegetables or whatever – use your imagination. It is helpful to choose a theme or culture, because then you can conduct research for more ideas.

START WITH A DOODLE

Doodling – drawing when your mind is occupied with other thoughts – is an immensely creative activity. Covering a page with random scribbles, strange creatures that grow of their own volition, patterns, lettering, objects and shapes will often contain the seed of an idea that can be nurtured and developed in a more "conscious" way later on. Doodle when you are on the phone, in meetings or while watching the television… the trick is not to be too aware of what you are doing. Look at the drawings afresh the next day to see what can be taken forward.

See where your pen takes you
The artist Paul Klee likened drawing to "taking a line for a walk". Doodling could be seen as letting your pen take your mind for a walk.

START WITH AN INCIDENT

Something may have happened to you today, yesterday or when you were little that you think is funny, poignant, or just plain strange. Keep a note of events like these to base ideas upon.

START WITH A FACT

Be it a startling piece of information, or just common knowledge, using something "real" from a news item or even a biology textbook can provide a starting point for a character or story.

Get to know your subject
Repeated studies of the same subject (in this case a rabbit, right) will lead you to notice things you might not otherwise have seen.

5 RESEARCH

Any intial idea that you have will need researching to enable you to develop it further into a picture-book concept.

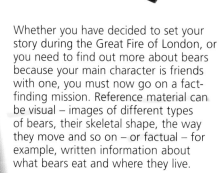

Whether you have decided to set your story during the Great Fire of London, or you need to find out more about bears because your main character is friends with one, you must now go on a fact-finding mission. Reference material can be visual – images of different types of bears, their skeletal shape, the way they move and so on – or factual – for example, written information about what bears eat and where they live.

Collected material
Gather your research material in a scrapbook or sketchbook. It doesn't have to be neat!

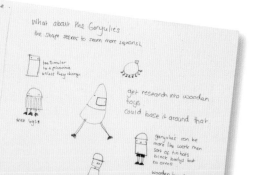

Starting points

"Research" does not mean typing a keyword into a search engine and waiting for 15,000 hits to come up. There are so many places that you can glean information from; don't limit yourself by relying on one method.

- **Libraries:** A good library will provide you will a wealth of different information sources from books to magazines and the internet.

- **Bookshops:** Try digging around in secondhand bookstores where the selection is likely to be more eclectic.

- **Magazines and newspapers:** Specialist magazines can offer a deeper or more up-to-date insight into a subject than reference books and are often highly illustrated.

- **Interviewing people:** You can find out a lot from talking to people and asking them to share their memories and knowledge.

TRY THIS

Inviting inspiration

Visit your local museum and forage until you find an artefact or room that inspires you. Document what you can while you are at the museum then, when you return home, find out as much as you can from other sources. Use your research to create a story containing the information, but told from an unusual perspective. For example, you could write about Egyptian mummification from a scarab beetle's point of view.

DEVELOPING A FEELING

Before you start the research, you might simply have a "feel" for a book idea, such as a mountainous setting or animal characters. Whatever you have to work with, finding out more about it will help you to develop the characters and storyline. You should know as much as possible about the characters, locations, clothes and historical period in general.

Even if the story is set in surroundings as familiar as your own kitchen, fill a sketchbook with drawings and photographs of the room and its contents. You may not need to use all the reference but your confidence and grasp of the subject will help you include the most relevant details to tell the story effectively.

VISUAL RESEARCH

Aesthetic considerations will also evolve around the visual research you undertake and the artists, colours, and techniques that you feel drawn to. A lot of the research process is instinctive and intuitive – you are simply analysing what you like and why. Gathering information together helps you see patterns and similarities in what you are drawn to. Remember that you are in charge of creating an entire world!

Reference material
Reference material can take the form of books, photographs, your own sketches (above and below right) – anything that will spark ideas and trigger memories relevant to your concept.

WEBSITES

Visual research

Sources of information are increasingly visual. There is an abundance of visual archives available online that can be incredibly inspiring and informative:

- **bibliodyssey.blogspot.com**
  This blog is updated constantly and gives access to the finest and strangest visual archives from libraries and museum collections around the world.

- **flickr.com**
  A searchable database of photographs (with varying permissions of use). Creative commons licenses allow limited appropriation of imagery; if an image is marked with a copyright symbol you can look but don't steal the idea – respect the owner's right to the image. Flickr is a great reference resource, and there are swathes of images from illustration groups and vintage children's books to look at.

Storing your research

The best practical advice when it comes to research is to store your material in a way that you can access easily. Paper files, digital folders or even a blog can be excellent repositories for your findings. Classifying the information will help you understand it better too, and will help you to identify patterns and themes in your preoccupations. Annotating your research – why you like a particular thing or what you would like to use it for – will also enhance the process.

Blogging

Many sites now offer free space for a blog (try eblogger. com or wordpress.org). The sign-up process is simple and uploading imagery and posting entries is not difficult. A blog is a robust way of storing and sharing research. It will enable you to categorize information and archive it by date. Over time you can build up a body of information.

MAKE IT MOVE
Pose, viewpoint, body language and even the media can all contribute
to a feeling of movement in an artwork (see page 40).

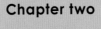

Chapter two

DEVELOPING AN IDEA

Essential reading for children's book illustrators, this section describes the key approaches to creating unique and memorable artwork that will stand out in a crowded marketplace; this is as much about developing your own style as it is about creating characters that appeal to particular age groups.

SKETCHBOOKS

Sketchbooks can have many different functions. They can be places for observation, doodles, notes and ideas; they provide a means for gathering visual information from the world in which you live.

TRY THIS

TRY THIS

Make sketching part of your routine

Get into the habit of drawing something in your sketchbook daily. It doesn't matter what you draw; more that you draw something every single day. It could be from observation, such as a self-portrait, family pet, kitchen worktop, the view out of a window, while traveling on a bus or train – in fact anything and everything around you is a potential subject.

Adopting this practice will help you to become comfortable with the habit of using sketchbooks; only then can it become a natural and instinctive process.

Drawing is fundamental to an illustrator and to create convincing images for your stories, you need to understand what you are drawing. Therefore gathering visual information and recording ideas, inspired by what you see and experience daily, helps to develop your drawing skills and creates the knowledge you need for further experimentation.

YOUR PERSONAL TOOLKIT

Sketchbooks are personal records that you will create for your own personal needs and interests in a way that suits you. The tools you choose to draw with will also depend on personal preference. The ideal sketching tools are easily portable and can be used instantly with no preparation, such as pencils, ballpoint pens, fountain pens and magic markers. (See pages 114 to 137 for more about media.) There are no rules dictating how to draw in your sketchbook; this will develop naturally the more you do it.

Pocket sketchbook
A small sketchbook is easy to carry around in your pocket or keep by the bed. A hard cover on your book will protect your work and give you something to lean on when drawing.

Sketchbooks are diverse in their shape, size, type of binding and quality of paper. Your choice will depend on your needs. A small, pocket-size sketchbook is good to keep by you at all times, to record everyday observations while on the move and develop creative thoughts and doodles. A larger sketchbook is useful for more leisurely observational studies and for use in developing your ideas and working through the design process.

CRASH COURSE

Shirley Hughes uses smooth, thin drawing paper to pencil out her images, then fibre-tip pen to fill them in, before proceeding to final artwork. Hughes feels that this loose, experimental stage allows her to observe unselfconsciously.

Sara Midda asserts that you can get ideas from anything, be it going to the shops or sitting in the garden. Her minute illustrations are crammed full of detail, a testament to the many aspects of the world her illustrator's mind absorbs.

Paper matters

Rough paper is textured and absorbent, great for washes of colour. Hot-pressed paper is smooth and non-absorbent, while cold-pressed paper (known as "not") has a texture that is smooth enough for detail. For drawing and painting, a versatile paper would be 140 lb (300 gsm) not.

7 OBSERVING CHILDREN

Some of the most successful authors and illustrators of children's books have a strong affinity with their audience. Contact with young children can be inspirational, and for some may be the most enjoyable part of the job.

You don't need to have a family of your own, but the observation of children can help enhance your illustration and writing. Subtle details taken from watching children give an honesty and sensitivity to your content – resulting in an altogether more convincing result. You may like to think that you remember what it is like to be a child, but it is only by watching how children eat, play and stand, for example, that you will truly be able to capture the realism of these actions.

Look at me

The sketch on the right reveals many details of this boy's character. His chest is thrust out and he wears his hat at a rakish angle, oozing confidence. He looks directly at his observer and, with his bare chest and feet, seems comfortable in his own skin. This illustration could only have been drawn from observation.

Drawing from life

Drawing family or children of friends is the easiest way to observe children. If they are asleep or watching television, you will have the opportunity to draw them when they are most likely to stay still for a time; however, this may not be the most interesting or quirky visually.

TRY THIS

Observe group behaviour

Try to observe children in a formal situation, such as a school play, ballet class or assembly. How do the children sit, stand and interact while they are supervised as a group, and supposedly on their best behaviour? What idiosyncrasies and personalities emerge? What do they do as their boredom levels (and potential for fidgeting) increase? Are any of them nose-picking or misbehaving? Such observations will prove useful for future reference. Make written notes if visual notes are difficult to achieve.

The relevance of observation and drawing children from life is strongly advocated in this book. However, this can be a particularly sensitive subject if the children are not your own. It may be necessary to have a criminal record check carried out, if you wish to approach or spend time with children in schools or playgroups for instance, particularly if the children are to be left unattended. Different institutions will have different policies. Take time to find out about these; you must observe them if you are to protect yourself from any anxieties or misinterpretation by guardians.

PHOTOGRAPHIC REFERENCES

There are reference books available that contain images of children in different poses. Such books provide useful reference material without the complication of copyright or criminal record check issues.

Lost in play
Children can be most charming when caught in the moment – either playing on their own (above) or helping mum bake a cake (left).

TIP

A criminal record check is not always transferable between different schools and institutions, so be aware of this if you wish to work with children in a range of environments.

CRASH COURSE

Any books illustrated by Shirley Hughes offer a wealth of reasons for why observing children can be worthwhile. An illustrator who has always recorded children in sketchbooks, she beautifully transfers her observations to creative, lively characterization. The sense of truth that comes through the drawings engages the reader in the reality of the everyday lives of the children.

Try the following:

The Big Alfie and Annie Rose Story Book
(1990)

Dogger
(1991)

Pencil and gouache
Like Shirley Hughes, this illustrator starts with a pencil drawing to create character and atmosphere. Then gouache is used, which has the softness of watercolour but a better density of colour.

8 MEDIA AND DRAWING STYLES

The range of techniques available to an artist is considerable. In response, there are many books available, from step-by-step techniques to analysis of contemporary professional examples. However, your own experimentation is the key to finding a comfortable and original method of working. The scale of the work will alter according to the technique; this is often difficult to appreciate when artwork is reduced and reproduced in a book.

TRY THIS

Compile a research file

Put together a research file of examples of artwork in categories of media, and shortlists of book prizes, competitions and so on. This can become unwieldy, so select only what is inspirational to you, or illustrates approaches you have never considered before.

Experiment

- Take a favourite image from your sketchbook and experiment with a wide range of materials, papers and technology to see how the image responds. Remember to change the scale according to the technique; larger scales will be necessary for broader tools, such as chalks or palette knives.
- Emphasize the line quality in some images, the shapes and mass in others.
- Keep to monochromatic colours so you can focus on the mark-making qualities and tone alone.

Brush, pen and coloured ink
The scale of the artwork is larger than some of the others due to the drawing tools used. Inks are more intense in colour than watercolour, so they can be used to create a much brighter result, or watered down to a tint.

Dip pen (and watercolour)
The quality of line varies in thickness as the pressure on the pen is altered. The scale is not large and this is one of the most popular forms of media for book illustration. Simple washes quickly turn drawings into colour artwork, so the drawing is of paramount importance.

Charcoal and watercolour
Charcoal smudges easily, so to combine it with watercolour the washes were applied first, and the black charcoal line was drawn on later to pull the form together.

Many artists without previous art-school experience feel nervous moving away from a drawing tool they have become familiar with, and may be disappointed if the results of new tools and media do not yield the same immediate success. The same applies to practicing or professional illustrators who need to rethink or freshen up their portfolio. But what if the same amount of practice given to your regular tool had been given to a different tool? Would it still seem so inept or cumbersome?

FINDING YOUR OWN STYLE

Developing a commercial style takes some research into what standards are already set by professional published artwork. What media is popular? What is the range of drawing styles and colour palettes used? What is deemed successful or trendy, and why? A critical eye is a useful requirement if you are to evaluate the success of your own work, and time is also needed to experiment with professional materials, colour, and black-and-white media.

CHOOSING YOUR MEDIUM

There is a wide range of media for the illustrator to choose from. If your drawing has an unusual or interesting quality to the line, or you particularly like to work in pen and ink, you may like to try working with transparent media, such as watercolour or dyes. Gutsy mark-making and confidence with colour may steer you to work with pastels, oil pastels, acrylics and mixed media, whereas graphic styles may be more suited to photography, collage and computerized manipulation in applications such as Photoshop. The list and combination of approaches, materials and surfaces to work with is endless. Have fun experimenting to find those that appeal the most.

Acylic
Generally used opaque, the paint has been built up here as washes on acrylic paper, giving a slightly textured appearance. Backgrounds should be painted first so the layers overlap to give a sense of depth to the finished piece.

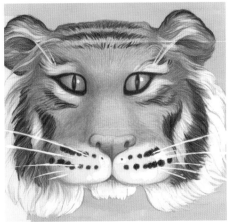

Coloured pencil crayon
Coloured pencil crayons can be used with strong, expressive marks, but also with precision and control, as shown here. A watercolour wash has been applied to provide a base to enhance the strength of the colour application over the top.

Pastel
Pastels generally need to be used on a fairly large scale. These soft pastels have been blended with a torchon and applied on watercolour paper tinted with a wash (although there are many pastel papers available to provide coloured grounds).

DEVELOPING YOUR OWN STYLE

Certain illustrators may inspire you to consider children's publishing as a career, but it is important first to develop a style that is original and instinctive. It is unlikely that publishers will tell you what they are looking for; they will just know it when they see it, so before trying to impress, look at your own abilities to find out what you enjoy and where your strengths lie.

CRASH COURSE

Quentin Blake has a spontaneous, scratchy style using pen and ink. His characters seep personalities that are eccentric and highly original, and his illustrations are immediately recognizable.

Victor Ambrus uses a combination of pencil and colour illustration – sometimes in the same piece of artwork – to fire people's imaginations about various historical eras.

ANALYZE YOUR STUDIES

If you are uncertain what you do best, take a good look at your sketchbooks. It is here that you are most likely to observe your natural visual response to ideas and imagery – when you are relaxed, spontaneous, experimental and uninhibited.

DON'T TRY TOO HARD

Try to avoid preconceived ideas of what drawing is; it is simply a method of recording information and does not need to be labour intensive. Don't view final artwork as something separate from what you do when you sketch or doodle. Many unpublished illustrators try too hard to produce "finished" artwork and images become overworked and static. All they need is to develop a personal style that feels as natural as handwriting.

Spontaneous doodles
Quick-fire sketches can reveal your strengths and weaknesses as an illustrator – and unlock the child within. Don't be afraid to sketch anything that pops into your mind; you may be on the path to your first illustrated story.

Fluid motion
A trip to the zoo initiated these beautiful, fluid pencil drawings that capture an extremely acute realism of the animals observed. Though conditioned to turn finished artwork into something laboured and static, the artist took time and care to retain the instinctive quality in her drawings.

Bold and simple
This artist developed her drawing style from successful studies she had made at a zoo, while experimenting with different drawing implements (above). Colour is secondary in her work; it is the strength of the calligraphic line and the convincing personalities of her characters that are her strengths.

The big picture
The lively, humorous characterization of these humans and animals (below) is mirrored by the artist's use of colour. Dry colour such as pastels and oil pastels showcased her talent, but initially required large surface areas to achieve the level of detail she sought to produce. However, she deliberately and successfully found a way to manage the size and scale of her work, maintaining the richness of colour and ensuring little was lost in reproduction.

Can you hear all kinds of dogs strolling along the promenade, smelling the fresh autumn air, enjoying the beautiful day? Listen, what else can you hear?

TRY THIS
Working on location
Take a range of materials and drawing tools to the zoo or a farm. It is important to draw at the location, and not just to take photographs as reference to work from. Do not be deterred by unfinished studies; these will still increase your confidence and improve your level of observation – providing excellent first-hand reference for anthropomorphism (see page 48). Such studies will also give you a true reflection of your strengths.

CRASH COURSE
Drawing for the Artistically Undiscovered by Quentin Blake and John Cassidy (1999)

Encyclopedia of Drawing Techniques by Hazel Harrison (1999)

Drawing with Colour by Judy Martin (1989)

These titles may help you reconsider the way you think about drawing, and also the tools that can be used for different approaches.

10

DEVELOPING CHARACTERS

To draw a character in a variety of situations as it moves through a narrative demands skill if the character is to remain believable, consistent, and attractive. The illustrator must be familiar with the character and really believe in it if they are to convince the reader.

ENGAGING THE READER

A successful character needs to charm and intrigue readers if they are to engage with it. A character doesn't necessarily have to be "cute" but it does have to be attractive or visually appealing in some way, because publishers generally put the it on the front cover and expect it to sell the book. Plus, merchandising, television rights and animation productions are always looking for interesting characters to use, so your subjects could become a lucrative opportunity. The more alluring the character, the more money there is to be made.

Characters may be thrust on you from an existing text and come with an author's background and setting. However, the character is often the starting point from which an author or illustrator finds inspiration to generate a story or, even better, a series.

The poor duck was sleepy and weepy and tired.

Animal characters
Helen Oxenbury shows deft characterizations in *Farmer Duck* (written by Martin Waddell). Every animal is uniquely represented through her drawing skills.

READ THIS

How to Write and Illustrate Children's Books and Get Them Published
by Treld Pelkey Bicknell and Felicity Trotman (1988)

Illustrating Children's Books: Creating Pictures for Publication
by Martin Salisbury (2004)

Then the cow and the sheep and the hens came back.

"Quack?" asked the duck.
"Moo!" said the cow.
"Baa!" said the sheep.
"Cluck!" said the hens.

Which told the duck the whole story.

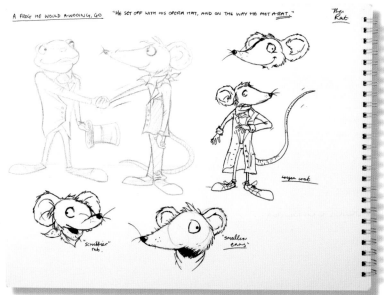

A FROG HE WOULD A-WOOING GO   "HE SET OFF WITH HIS OPERA HAT, AND ON THE WAY HE MET A RAT."   The Rat

"scrubber" rat

"smaller ears"

larger coat

Personality pointers

A handshake, a grin, a nervous glance; all of these reveal personality.

FINDING INSPIRATION

Inspiration for characters may come from people you already know, or from observing children from life or reference. What is the "profile", or personality, of your character? Does he or she have hobbies, family and friends? Not all of this information may be relevant to your story but will help to create an individual. Clothes, shoes, props and hairstyles all contribute to the identity. Nothing can be overlooked.

Mapping it out

Mind maps allow your thoughts to roam free and make their own connections. Using this tool you can create a character full of quirks.

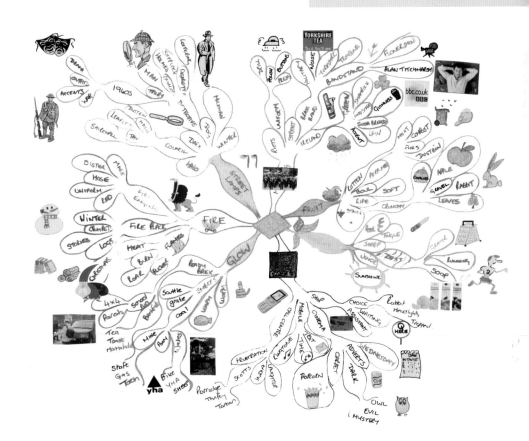

PRESENTING YOUR WORK

Even when an artist finds a character they like and develops it through artwork in their portfolio, it may be a sketch among the development work in a sketchbook that takes the interest of an art director, rather than a more resolved outcome.

Most publishers would only commission an illustrator they believe to have potential to produce character sheets, before giving them a book to complete. This enables the publisher to assess the character's appeal and the consistency of the artist, and the process may continue for some time. This work is usually paid, but offers no guarantee of a complete project.

The eyes have it
Seven sketches, one difference – the eyes. These sketches reveal how telling one single detail can be in the characterization of an animal.

Face value
Which of these faces is the most appealing? It is only by experimenting that you will find a character and a look to satisfy publishers and readers.

Moving pictures
Practise drawing your character in action, as well as in static poses. The character below is full of personality – not least because of the humorous interaction with her pet.

Most appealing children's characters:

- *Charlie and Lola*, Lauren Child
  (first book published 1999)

  Charlie and Lola feature in a series of books by Lauren Child. Big brother Charlie has his hands full with his energetic sister, Lola, as she copes with different situations such as going to bed, a wobbly tooth and food she doesn't like.

- *The Snowman*, Raymond Briggs
  (1985)

  Raymond Briggs' beautiful illustrations create a character that children and adults immediately fall in love with. There are no words in this story.

- *Mr. Men* and *Little Miss*, Roger Hargreaves
  (*Mr. Men* first published 1971; *Little Miss* first published 1981)

  With simple, humorous drawings covering over 90 characters, Hargreaves manages to create a set of characters that make adults and children smile.

- *The Cat in the Hat*, Dr. Seuss
  (1957)

  If you're looking for a chaotic but likeable main character, then this is the cat for you. The manic Cat in the Hat arrives, disrupts, tidies up and leaves again. What more could a child ask for in a friend?

- *The BFG*, Roald Dahl
  (1982)

  The ink lines and watercolours of Quentin Blake's illustrations create a giant who is huge and scary, but also kind and friendly. Like Sophie in the story of the BFG, readers can discover that friends come in the most unexpected sizes and shapes.

Character: the sidekick

Age: in the first book, 11. Ages a year per book

Appearance: blond hair, green eyes, chip in front tooth, freckles in summer

Characteristics: quiet, observing, gently guides the main character towards the right decision

Family: divorced parents, lives with mother and sister

Catchphrase: Look out!

Animated animals

Howling, sniffing, rolling, bristling; animal actions speak volumes. But if you can't get these right on the page, your story will fall down. Practice and observation will bring your animal characters to life.

Character checklists

When you need to keep track of your characters over several books, it is essential to keep checklists of all their traits. This will save you time and errors – and keep your favourite characters alive in your imagination.

Character: the girl spy

Age: 12. Stays the same age in each book

Appearance: coal-black hair, tall for her age, wears glasses

Characteristics: inquisitive, clever, sometimes clumsy, nose for a mystery, overenthusiastic

Family: lives alone with her parents

Catchphrase: Cover me, I'm going in!

11 PROPORTION

The age of a character is very difficult to get right. Your story may include a range of different ages, which must remain consistent and believable throughout the book. Correct proportion is key to portraying characters of particular ages.

CHECKING PROPORTIONS

For accurate representations, checking proportions of the body against the face and head is the most common measuring tool, although posture will also make a difference. Character studies that investigate possible poses and viewpoints may use a framework composed of shapes (see opposite). This will help you to calculate how perspective and action poses will alter the proportions. Reference to these shapes, or even the proportions of a stick-like figure, can help a character remain consistent.

SCALE

The scale of children both next to objects and within differing environments can only be improved if you familiarize yourself with everyday situations using your sketchbook. For more realistic illustrations, photographs can be used as a reference.

Head height
This diagram shows how the proportion of a human body in relation to the head changes over time. The number of heads that make up a standing figure differ with age.

| **0 to 2 years** | **4 to 6 years** | **6 to 8 years** | **12 to 14 years** | **18 to 20 years (Male)** | **18 to 20 (Female)** |
| 4 heads | 5.75 heads | 6.25 heads | 7.25 heads | 7.5 heads | 7.5 heads |

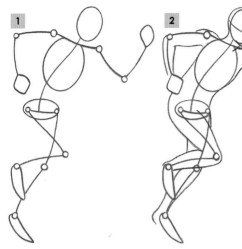

FRAMEWORK OF SHAPES

Using a framework of shapes to position a figure in a pose helps you to consider balance, movement and poise before committing to a more time-consuming rendition of a character. "Opening up" the space between arms and legs when trying to capture motion creates more interesting silhouettes and negative spaces.

BABIES

Babies are notoriously difficult to draw. It is important to remember that the mask of a baby's face is only a very small proportion of the overall sphere of the head.

1. On the move
The slight exaggeration of a pose makes it more expressive. Tilting the shoulders or the position of the body forwards generates movement. Giving the upper body something to do makes a pose less static.

2. Fleshing out
Once you have established the pose and are happy with the effect, you can start to apply the outlines of the body around the basic framework of shapes.

TRY THIS

Fleshing out the framework

Draw with soft, versatile media such as charcoal or graphite sticks to build up drawings of children from photographic reference, viewing them as mannequins and imagining limbs and ribcages where they are covered by clothing. Re-dress this framework with different clothes, shoes and hair, maintaining the child's original posture and shape.

Now try the same exercise with an older child, and finally an adult. Note the differences.

Drawing practice

- Two- to five-minute poses in life classes will help to build up confidence in your ability to observe quickly and accurately. This also gives you the chance to experiment with drawing tools and media that produce fluid, precise and descriptive lines. Practise recording the human form in different ways, concentrating on mass and contours. This will help to finely tune your ability to observe information.

- Try drawing figures of all ages from the television, making a note of their approximate age. This should give you access to a wide source of ages and builds, helping you to depict human form accurately. Remember to use drawing tools that enable the line to flow quickly and freely.

READ THIS

The Complete Drawing and Sketching Course by Stan Smith (2002)

Figures and Faces: A Sketcher's Handbook by H. Laidman (1979)

Find your flair!
In this illustration from *We're Going on a Bear Hunt,* Helen Oxenbury's simple and attractive style appears in her drawings of wide-limbed and rounded-feature children. What's your style?

12 EXPRESSION

The slightest change of expression on the face tells the reader a lot about the way a character is feeling. Using the characters' features to show emotions will enhance and strengthen your narrative.

CHANGING MOODS

Changing the expressions of characters within a story – even subtly – helps to depict the facets of their personalities and their changes of mood from page to page. However, altering the proportions of a face to show expression while keeping the face consistent can be difficult. Most illustrators would expect to explore emotional characterization as a range of studies before embarking on a book. Being able to draw the face in profile and from other angles is important too; remember that a face should not always look out of the page if you want its owner to engage with other characters.

Body gestures

Don't just think about the face – everything about the body language of a character helps to convey a sense of its unique personality.

Get the eyes right

Using pupils and eyelids enables an artist to take complete control of the expression of the eyes. It becomes possible to open the eyes to show shock, or close them to squint. Eyebrows also contribute significantly.

Smug

Disgusted

Warm

Content

Dazed

Scope for expression

Whether the eyes and mouth are open or closed, small or large, or even if the position of the head is altered, even the simplest of faces can show a range of expressions.

TRY THIS

Think of a nursery rhyme with an incident that requires you to consider a strong emotion for the character concerned, for example Little Bo Peep or Little Miss Muffet. Illustrate the essence of the situation, trying to focus on and capture what the character is going through and how they might feel – surprised, frightened, happy or sad. Don't be satisfied with the first image that comes into your head! Rework the drawings next to each other on a large sheet of paper so you can compare the drawings and see which you think are most successful. Play around with the poem too – if you enjoy writing – twisting the scenario to create alternative situations and possibly emotions.

Exploring character

Exploring the facial expressions of your characters (below left) is a good way to get to know them and consider their personalities. Faces change as the brow, jaw and muscles in the cheeks around the mouth are altered by expressions.

Dots for eyes

"Dots for eyes" is currently a very popular solution, but can limit the amount of expression you can generate in a face without careful consideration. Large, googly, cartoon eyes are often unpopular with publishers, despite the success of manga and Disney, but keep watching the market trends as this can change.

Restricting expression to the face limits its impact; body language naturally supports it. Don't forget the hands as they add to the impression. They need to fit proportionately with the size and style of the figure and not be deliberately hidden away, even if they are difficult to draw.

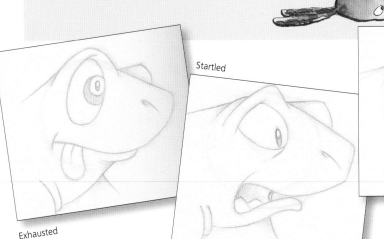

Exhausted

Startled

Sheepish

Disheartened

13 MOVEMENT

In an illustration, movement must be captured in a single, static pose. Considering the options throughout an action, stage-by-stage, like an animator line-testing, can help you to deliver the most effective moment "frozen in time".

IMPRESSIONS OF MOVEMENT

Selecting the pose, viewpoint, body language, expression and even the media or technique all contribute to the effect of movement. Media with fluid lines, such as dip pens or brushes, make expressive marks that are ideal for suggesting movement in the drawing.

The overall compositional design may include props and objects that help to strengthen the association with movement, such as trees swaying, cloth billowing, hair lifted or scarves blowing – but take care to make sure they all move in the same direction!

Lines of movement
Here, the sense of movement portrayed through the positioning of limbs and features is accentuated by lines of movement around the relevant parts.

Speed
The hair streaming out behind this character creates a strong sense of movement at speed.

Up   Down

Choose a pose that not only tells the story, but also makes interesting shapes that will add to your design. Imagine the figure silhouetted. Could the shape look more interesting if a limb were extended away from the body or the angle of view changed slightly? Shadows on the ground suggest something up in the air. Movement lines around comic styles can sometimes work, but don't overdo them.

Economy
Use everything about an image to demonstrate its state of movement – shape, colour and line. Make all the elements work together to convey the message.

Inflate   Burst

Props
Here, the rug beneath the characters adds to the sense of movement in the image without directly contributing to the movement in a physical way.

TRY THIS

Using a child character you have developed, imagine what would happen if they were playing with an inflated balloon. Try to think of how they would chase it, hit it, catch it, jump with it and so on as a series of figure studies on a large sheet of paper. Eventually start to format the drawings to consider composition and how angles and cropping can affect the relationship between the child and the balloon, giving a sense of space and action.

The importance of reference

Creating an unintentionally static image is often the result of relying solely on secondhand reference. If you observe figures or animals from life, the chances are they will be moving (drawing at the zoo, people walking in the street or children playing on the beach, for example). The simplified sketched outlines and shapes of the action taking place – even if incomplete – will trigger memories of what you saw. In this way a drawing can act as a reminder of something that has been observed and understood.

14
BABIES AND TODDLERS

One of the most difficult types of character to draw convincingly, and yet still keep attractive, is a baby. The proportions of babies and toddlers are often unfamiliar to draw and you will need to observe and consider them carefully.

READ THIS

Tickle, Tickle
by Helen Oxenbury (1987)

Helen Oxenbury draws young children and babies in a simple and attractive style with wide limbs and rounded features that are familiar to this age group.

Peepo
by Janet and Allan Ahlberg (1983)

How to be a Little Sod
by Tony Ross (1999)

KNOWING YOUR SUBJECT

Knowing very young children, or having your own, can be a distinct advantage if you intend to illustrate for this age group – as reference, or as inspiration for stories and characters. Understanding young behaviour, and appreciating how quickly babies develop into toddlers, will help you create convincing characters and situations. There are plenty of books that identify stages of development of young children if your access to babies is limited.

There are wonderful clothes, furniture and other props associated with babies and very young children – dummies, beakers, teddies, blankets, bibs and pushchairs – and the way the child interacts with these items will affect its body language and behavior. Catalogues or websites from shops selling baby products may provide much visual reference, but it may be worth spending time drawing a real pushchair, for example, no matter how simple. The smallest of details can make your drawing believable.

Shining through
A good baby illustration reveals a personality that shines through from the earliest age. One look at this baby's eyes reveals a friendly soul and a glimmer of cheekiness.

TRY THIS

Collect a number of baby catalogues and magazines for reference (below), and books on baby development to inspire ideas for narratives. Develop baby and toddler characters and combine them with a prop in each pose you draw. Consider the narrative in the situations you are portraying. For example, a child can wear coloured sunscreen and eat ice cream while sitting in a pushchair with the parasol up. Or perhaps he sits on a potty looking at a book.

Best books for babies and toddlers:

■ *The Very Hungry Caterpillar* by Eric Carle (1969)

This is the simple story of how a caterpillar eats and eats until he is transformed into a cocoon and then into a butterfly. Children are presented with a character that faces the same challenge they do: growing up. Carle uses beautiful collage artwork and die-cut holes in the pages.

■ *Guess How Much I Love You* by Sam McBratney and Anita Jeram (1995)

Little Nut Brown Hare and Big Nut Brown Hare find unusual ways of showing how much they love each other. For anyone who finds it difficult to put emotions into words, this is an innocent look at different ways of expressing how you feel – with a lovely surprise at the end.

■ *Don't Put Your Finger In the Jelly, Nelly!* by Nick Sharratt (1993)

Nick Sharratt's thick lines and bright, simple colours are not dissimilar to the way a child might draw. In this picture book the rhymes and wordplay entertain alongside visual jokes. Die-cut holes in the pages cry out for a small hand to put a finger through them.

■ *Where the Wild Things Are* by Maurice Sendak (1963)

First published in 1963, this is the story of a boy who gets sent to bed without any tea because he's behaved like such a monster. Max's angry imagination transforms his bedroom into a jungle and he goes out to meet other Wild Things. The story allows Max – and young readers – to experience the highs and lows of extreme emotion.

■ *Sylvester and the Magic Pebble* by William Steig (1969)

Beautiful watercolour pictures illustrate a story that follows Sylvester, a little donkey, and his adventures with a magic pebble that makes his wishes come true. The book explores difficult emotions such as loneliness and sadness. The story ends happily, but helps children understand that the world is full of many emotions – not all of them lovely, but all of them important.

What do they have in common?

Something unexpected: unusual ways to say "I love you", made-up words, jungles in bedrooms and a donkey who makes wishes. With picture-book writing, the only rule is to use your imagination.

BABY AND TODDLER CHARACTERISTICS

Babies and young children typically have round heads and tummies and chubby, short hands. The forehead protrudes slightly and seems very high when there is little hair, while the chin recedes. It's possible to emphasize the eyes – they are the same size as an adult's, but in a smaller skull – but better to understate or even ignore eyebrows. These are generally so fair they can hardly be seen. Noses are small, and upper lips more prominent than lower.

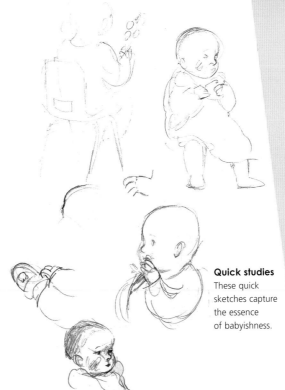

Body language
A simple drawing of a crawling child with her nappy peeking out and her dummy in the corner of her mouth displays fun and humour.

Quick studies
These quick sketches capture the essence of babyishness.

Typical developmental stages

■ **3 months:** lifting their heads while lying on their fronts

■ **3–5 months:** reaching out for objects

■ **5 months:** handling objects

■ **6 months:** sitting up without support; starting to crawl; pulling themselves up on furniture

■ **10 months+:** starting to walk

■ **14 months:** starting to feed themselves

■ **18 months:** starting to kick or throw a ball

■ **2 years:** learning to ride a bike

15 BOYS AND GIRLS

Finding a method or style for drawing figures is one hurdle; giving them a personality and identity is quite another. But when you take time to consider the trials and tribulations of growing up, it is easier to generate stories and create characters with which the reader can sympathize.

CHARACTER PROFILING

When representing young children it is easy to resort to generalizations: boys get up to mischief, are less focused on schoolwork and interact more physically; girls are gentler, demonstrate maternal instincts and throw tantrums. Profiling the children in your illustrations will help you to remain focused on the characters you wish to portray. Love or hate your characters, but never feel indifferent towards them!

Playing with cliché

A checklist like the one below helps you to play with clichés and subvert them. Can you create a child character that challenges the norm?

Character profile checklist:
The little sister who knows more than you do.
The bully who goes home and cries.
The best friend you don't always like.
The naughty boy who's clumsy.
The perfect girl who picks her nose in private.
The other child you say you hate, but secretly like.

Playful outfits

Dressing up as a bee, a fairy or a Native American – fancy dress allows children to explore different sides to themselves.

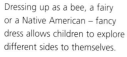

REFLECTING DIVERSITY

An illustrator needs to reflect the multicultural society we live in, particularly in non-fiction. Publishers in many countries will demand that this is taken into consideration. Remember though, that characterization of different races is a sensitive issue. You will need good reference to enable you to portray features accurately and in a way that personifies a culture yet without causing offense. Representing religious beliefs other than your own and children with special needs are further considerations.

Child characteristics

As children grow older, they develop more individual features.

The eyebrows and the shape of the nose and mouth become more distinctive. The head is still fairly large in proportion to the body, on a skinny neck and narrow shoulders.

There are interesting hairstyles to consider now, as well as an opportunity for pathos and humour!

FIRST EXPERIENCES

Consider your own experiences of doing something for the first time, or recollect any other significant childhood experiences. Many such events are serious issues for children, and reading a story that enables them to talk about it or hear the perspective from someone else can be of great support and comfort. Examples include: going to the dentist, school or hospital for the first time; dealing with bullying; coping with death of a pet or a relative; and understanding where babies come from.

OLDER CHARACTERS

If you have the ability to draw older children, include black and white illustrations of them in your portfolio; you may receive commissions for storybooks and non-fiction. There is also a market for the illustration of children's books for reluctant readers – featuring older characters but not text-heavy – in which comic-style storyboarding plays a more significant role.

Convincing characters
Sketching children at play can help you convince publishers that you have the eye and sensitivity to paint compelling pictures for your audience.

All about firsts
An outdoor swim can be a memorable experience for a child. You could feature this type of event in your story.

Child development stages

- **3 years:** Children can catch a large ball, ride a tricycle and finger-paint. An action-filled illustrated book full of fun activities such as these would engage a young reader.

- **4 years:** What do young children and rabbits have in common? They can both hop! Could you write a story using these two ingredients?

- **5 years:** Children play at make-believe and enjoy dressing up. They can walk on tiptoe. What about a story where a child dresses in costume and tiptoes over to scare his mother?

16 ADULTS

A common trap to fall into when illustrating adult characters is repeating old clichés: a granny with grey hair in a bun and wearing glasses; a family consisting of a mother, father, girl, boy and dog; the mother staying home while the father goes out to work. Challenge any of these stereotypical portrayals by first asking yourself: is this really the case in today's society?

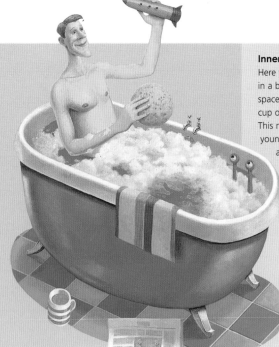

Inner child
Here you can see a grown man in a bubble bath, playing with a space rocket, his newspaper and cup of tea forgotten on the floor. This makes him appealing to young readers and teaches them an important early lesson: inside all of us is a child.

Same difference
The same illustrator, but four very different women. Dressed in tweed or platform sandals, there are no rules for the older generation.

KEEPING IT REAL

Grandparents can be agile and fashionable, and these days they are often involved with raising their grandchildren. Many mothers go out to work and have careers, so childcare plays a much greater role in the life of their child than in previous generations. Equally, fathers often do the vacuumcleaning or prepare the food.

Cultural mixes within families are more common then ever before, as are single parent families. Same-gender relationships are now also entering the equation. The media plays a big part in educating children about the different relationships in society and they tend to accept the changes common to their generation quite naturally. Any preconceptions need to be considered and challenged if books are to reach out to a wider audience. Ambiguity in all aspects of life is possibly more attractive than ever before.

Old and young
Older characters and young readers have much in common – both are outside of the workaday world, free to play and create.

Face studies
Sketches reveal the subtle details that age can add to a variety of adult faces.

FINDING REFERENCE

Inspiration for characters may come from observing people you already know or from printed or online reference sources. Clothes, shoes, props and hairstyles all contribute to a unique identity. Take time to research all of this carefully; nothing should be overlooked!

Draw on the familiar
Faces you have seen every day of your life may present unexpected surprises if you take the time to draw them.

Engaging adult characters:

- *Father Christmas*
  by Raymond Briggs (1973)

  This version of Father Christmas challenges children's expectations – he's grumpy! Just like some other grown-ups young readers might know…

- *Mr Large in Charge*
  by Jill Murphy (2005)

  A series of books in which elephant parents clumsily try to look after their family. Mr and Mrs Large show that non-human parents might not always get it right, but they do care.

- *The Adventures of Asterix*
  by René Goscinny and Albert Uderzo (first published as a series of comic books in 1959)

  Originally the star of a series of French comics, the diminutive Asterix continues to appeal to children of all ages today in many different publishing formats.

17 ANTHROPOMORPHISM

Animal characters imbued with human characteristics have featured in many stories for children.
They crop up in fables, myths and legends, representing the extremes of human behaviour and reinforcing the century-old stereotypical characteristics for certain animals. Crucially, the use of anthropomorphized animals in a story enables the illustrator to depict a situation without any particular reference to age, social standing, gender or race.

Best anthropomorphic characters:

- *Duck in the Truck*
  by Jez Alborough (2000)
  The interaction, expression and body language between these characters leaves the audience in no doubt as to what is happening.

- *Kipper and Roly*
  by Mick Inkpen (2001)
  This mischievous character has huge appeal in his design, humour and cuddle factor. The characters are simple, sensitive interpretations.

- *Olivia*
  by Ian Falconer (2000)
  This very original interpretation of a little pig, with the trademark limited palette, captures the personality of a little girl. The movement and expression translate to human behaviour exactly.

DRAWING FROM LIFE

Attributing human characteristics to an animal is a great deal easier if you have a really good understanding of the animal concerned. Studying an animal from life is by far the best way to develop an original character with a "real" sense of movement, posture and personality. Any other visual sources will need to show a variety of positions and provide some insight into the animal's behaviour. Studying film might be a possible source of reference for understanding an animal's skeletal structure and the way it moves.

PET APPEAL

The close relationship between humans and their pets makes these animals ideal for tackling sensitive issues. The "ahhhh" factor of an especially cute animal will also help to sell your product. Many animals are colourful, or exude personality, and for lots of new illustrators, these can be easier to draw! Children will always love a well designed animal character and the appeal of animals is universal.

Donkey
A four-legged animal stands and skates like a human. Its features are relatively accurate, though the expressions and movement are not.

Four legs to two
The ball-socket and lines drawn to represent the limbs preserve the consistency of the proportions of the character and help you confidently manipulate the pose.

TRY THIS

A 180-degree rotation of a character study – known as a "turnaround" – is part of the initial development process in animation. The lengths of limbs and so on are lined up as the figure turns, usually in a standing pose. Try this yourself as an interesting way of establishing the proportions of an anthropomorphized character, whether the animal is zoologically correct or has a human body with an animal's head.

If you favour a more spontaneous style generated from doodles, test for consistency by repeating your character a number of times next to each other moving from left to right along a horizontal line.

EXPANDING ON THE REFERENCE

When using good photographic reference, it can be helpful to break the animal down into simple shapes or a sticklike figure to learn the essential proportions. View the animal's structure as though it were transparent, using the position of ball joints to help you extend limbs from the torso with accurate lengths in changing positions.

Just as it can help to think of the structure of an animal as a transparent form, the same can be applied to placing the character in situations, such as driving a car or sitting on a chair. Draw the object in perspective first, then draw the character sitting on it or in it. (This is more likely to give a convincing end result than the other way around.)

Badger
Here's a selection of anthropomorphized poses.

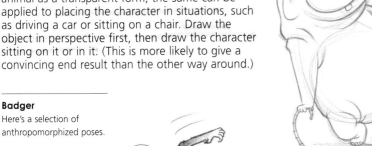

The arms and outstretched "hands" exaggerate the wailing.

Tilting the body and lifting the limbs gives an impression of marching forward.

The shadow shows that both feet are off the ground.

Rotation
Drawing the features and limbs as the figure turns helps you familiarize yourself with the character as a three-dimensional object. The repetition also establishes the proportions.

18 FIGURE AND GROUND

When illustrators talk about "figure and ground," they are talking about composition – the relationship between the various characters in the story and their relationship to the situation or environment in the text.

Foreground
In this image, there is only foreground, entirely occupied by the severely cropped character, creating an extreme sense of presence and closeness.

VISUAL INTERPRETATION

Imagine you control the situation like a stage or film set, using the same technical language as would be used in animation and live action. So, you have a foreground, a middleground and a background in which to move your characters around, trying to achieve the best visual interpretation of a particular scene.

Where you place characters and objects within a given layout on a page, exploiting the depth of field, adds to the impact of the storytelling. There is a variety of ways to help create a three-dimensional illusion for the characters to move through: overlapping, perspective, scale and placement all heighten the effect and interpretation of the text. Emotionally the child needs to be able to engage with what is seen and what is read. This is affected not only by the placement of characters in the right place within the depth of field, but also through the expression and body language of the characters.

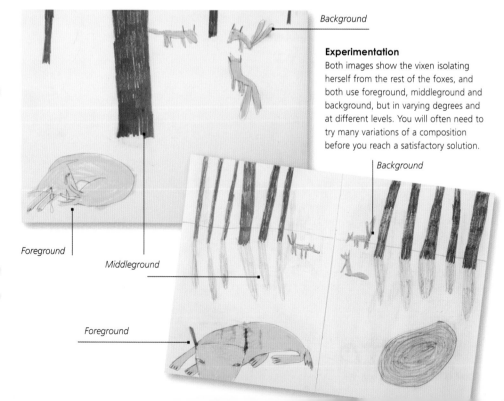

Background

Foreground

Middleground

Background

Foreground

Experimentation
Both images show the vixen isolating herself from the rest of the foxes, and both use foreground, middleground and background, but in varying degrees and at different levels. You will often need to try many variations of a composition before you reach a satisfactory solution.

Compositional proportions

You are in control of the aesthetic aspects of your composition. A useful guideline is the "Golden Section" in which a line or rectangle is divided into two parts so that the ratio of the smaller to the larger is equal to the ratio of the larger to the whole line. This ratio (approximately 8:3) has been known since antiquity, and was believed to possess inherent aesthetic virtues, bringing art and nature into harmony. You don't need to slavishly follow the principle, and anyway your format may not allow it. But the basic rules are always worth bearing in mind: the picture surface shouldn't be divided symmetrically; figures should not be placed in the centre of your paper; a fence should not be positioned so it runs horizontally across your illustration, equally dividing the distance from the bottom edge of your drawing to the horizon line. Of course, there are no rules that can't broken.

1 Construct a unit square (red outline).
2 Draw a line from the midpoint of one side to an opposite corner.
3 Use that line as the radius to draw an arc that

defines the long dimension of the rectangle.
4 You can go on dividing the resulting space into ever smaller proportional units (see above).

In practice
Three examples showing characters or focal points positioned on the golden intersection; the last one works from the left and right.

Breaking rules
Top, a formal centred composition; above, an anarchic, tightly cropped composition, in keeping with the subject matter.

Viewpoint

Viewpoint is the position that you choose for the reader to view an illustration. Viewpoint can have a dramatic effect on composition and mood. Above, a simple standing-height, eye-level viewpoint. Right, an extreme viewpoint and dizzying perspective give a sense of enclosure and movement from the ground up towards the treetops. The bird occupies the foreground; the owl is flying out of the middleground and the figure is a tiny presence on the forest floor. This composition creates an illusion of great size and scale. As you look down from one of the towering trees, you feel right at the centre of the action.

Sturdy trunks stand short and tall. A trunk supports the body of a tree, like your legs support your body.

19
FRAMES AND BORDERS

Many illustrators use decorative elements and "ornaments" that sit outside the main narrative illustrations to elucidate and elaborate on the story. These can add atmosphere or contain symbolic details from the story.

When you tell a story using images, every element in the story becomes iconic to some degree. In the same way that the relationship between individual words in a poem subtly redefines their meaning in accordance with the overall message and tone of the poem, so too do the images in a picture book work together to create the overall meaning of the book. The representation of objects, animals, clothing and even colours will accrue meaning as the imagery progresses, and repeated use will draw attention to their significance.

Girl and rabbit
The delicate, detailed line drawing naturally fits within an oval format. The vignette is enhanced by the shape of the border and the subtle colours in the tiny flowers.

CRASH COURSE

Famous examples of frames and borders:

- **Jane Ray**
  Her rich, stylized and highly decorative illustrations are often associated with her use of gold.

- **Jan Pienkowski**
  Famous for his silhouettes – the intricate outlines enhance the pages alongside full-colour work.

- **Nicola Bailey**
  The main illustrations are watercolours, applied with a pointillist technique. Borders balance the design.

Visual integration
Whether your borders add to the story or simply act as a decorative device, they should integrate with the main artwork and are often produced as part of it.

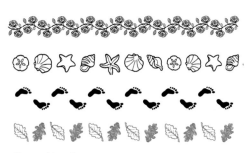

Themed borders
Your borders don't simply have to be decorative; they could add a narrative element as well. Here, festive fairy lights form a whimsical border (below); on another page, a row of stockings are hung up for Christmas Eve (below left).

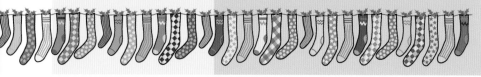

NAVIGATIONAL CLUES

If you look at very old illuminated manuscripts such as the *Book of Kells*, the distinction between the border and the body text becomes unclear, with marginalia offering interpretations on the text. Historically borders were a way of breaking up the monotony of the printed page, with ornaments used as chapter headings. These also served to give a visual clue to the content of that section of the book and so helped the reader navigate backwards and forwards in a large text. In picture books today the use of frames and borders in the design often signals a more traditional type of book.

Book of Kells
The beginning of the summary of the Gospel according to Matthew features elaborate decoration of the page, including images and figures within the intense pattern framework. The labored, indulgent use of detail and gold shows the importance of the piece of work.

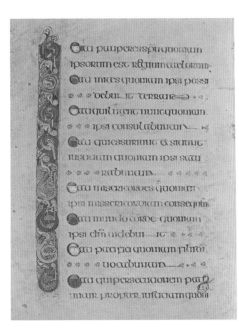

Helen Shoesmith's illustrations for *The Secret Garden*
By highlighting some of the iconic imagery in the story of *The Secret Garden* by Frances Hodgson Burnett, Helen Shoesmith draws attention to the importance of small things in the narrative – a key, a robin, a flower – these are all catalysts for the action and also represent the themes of secrecy, loss and the regenerative qualities of being among natural things. The stifling, dark, oppressive world of the house is contrasted with the light and airy drawings of the garden, and the frames and borders use imagery to reinforce these concepts.

Colour plates

The traditional look of a book designed with frames and borders is a result of the way books used to be produced. Before colour printing was the norm, illustrated books had colour plates that were inserted after the book was printed. The border was printed in black with the rest of the text, and showed where the plate was to go. The borders created visual harmony by connecting the colour illustrations with the overall design of the book.

TRY THIS

Commentaries

- Take small details from your story and work up a series of border "commentaries" on the main text.

- Comment, for example, on the mice and pumpkin in Cinderella before they are transformed, or the mirror and apple in *Snow White* or any detail in your story that you feel is significant – bus tickets, shoes, burnt toast, whatever! Look at creating small "spot" type illustrations, and also see if you can work them into a decorative border about 5 cm (2 in) wide. You need only work up two sides of the border, as the rest can be generated digitally from your artwork.

Chapter three

TELLING
THE STORY

This section explores the techniques that writers and illustrators use to tell an engaging story, spur the narrative along and encourage readers to keep turning the pages.

TIGER, TIGER
Varying the size and crop of visuals on a page can encourage page-turning habits in young readers (see page 82).

20 STORY STRUCTURE

Most fiction stories – from children's picture books to adult novels – have the same basic structure. You will find this structure in everything from ancient Greek myths to the latest Hollywood blockbuster.

Planning for the future

Writing a novel can be isolating and dispiriting, especially if you take the wrong turn in your story and then have to abandon several chapters and thousands of words. The more you plan your story before you write it, the less likely this is to happen. That's not to say you can't deviate from your initial plan. All writers find fresh ideas as their story unfurls. But just writing a story with no clear idea where your characters are going to end up is a recipe for hours of wasted work.

THEME

All fiction invariably has a theme, and it usually involves your main character – the protagonist – overcoming adversity. This can be anything from beating playground bullying to saving the world. Within the theme there is often a moral – such as "working together is better than acting alone", or "doing bad things causes unhappiness to both the perpetrator and others". Although adult fiction writers sometimes write stories with an ambiguous or dubious theme, if you are writing for children you will need to produce a story with a clear and positive moral. It would be an unusual children's publisher who produced a book suggesting that crime does pay, or that bullying is fun and makes you feel good about yourself.

MOTIVATION

Once you've established your setting – where the action takes place – you will need a cause: something that is happening or has happened to make your characters behave as they do. For example: Molly's mother is sick but too poor to pay for medicine; Charlie's best friend Ivan has gone missing. The cause drives the story forwards.

ACTION AND ANTAGONISM

How your characters act in response to the motivating "cause" provides the "effect", or action, of the story. So, Molly will try to raise money for her mother; Charlie will search for his friend. In most stories your character's actions will be thwarted by an antagonist – your book's central "baddie", who is trying to stop your hero achieving their aim. Your antagonist could be a person or thing, for example, a classroom rival, the Gestapo or even the weather. Without an antagonist it will be difficult to create suspense, and your reader will become bored with the story.

BUILDING TO A CLIMAX

All the excitement, suspense, concern, and trepidation in your story has to build to a crescendo. This is the part where all seems lost for your hero – they think their friends are dead and are just about to be murdered themselves by your central antagonist! This should be the part of the story where the reader finds it especially impossible to put the book down. Make sure your crescendo or climax comes close to the end of the book.

THE RIGHT ENDING

The end of the story provides the resolution. It is a brave writer who gives the story an unhappy ending, especially in children's fiction. Your reader will be drawn into your book because they like your main character or characters. They want to feel their struggles have been worthwhile and that all is well in the world when the story ends.

How to write a story plan

- Before you start planning your story, you probably already know what it's going to be about. Try to write two sentences that sum up the story:

  "When Sarah and Rosie take a ride on the ghost train, they discover that they don't have to pay money to be scared. The ghost ride takes them down dark tunnels to another world where a terrifying question faces the girls: how will they get home?"

  If you find that you're struggling to summarize, you may have a problem with your story.

- From here, sketch out your plan. Make a bulleted list of what you want your story to achieve, and by when.

- Next, write up the story plan. It's a good idea to write this plan in the first tense: *"Sarah and Rosie meet outside the gates…"* This will prevent the plan from morphing into the actual manuscript.

- Avoid inserting dialogue into the story plan. But do think about where and when dialogue will appear.

- Try to have a sense of where chapter breaks will fall. You will need good, strong chapter endings to drive the story on. By this stage, the plan allows you to see any weak spots. Do you have acres of solid dialogue? Does a character spend too much time thinking? Where are the secondary characters? Does the logic of your story make sense? A story plan will highlight these and other issues. Remember, the story plan is the blueprint for your manuscript – rush past this stage at your peril.

The point of view stays with Sarah at all times. You will need to decide what your narrative perspective is going to be.

The story stays in the present tense throughout.

The beginnings of narrative tone are emerging – there are moments of humour. This is a stage at which you can decide the tone your story is going to take.

There are regular references to Sarah's emotions as she moves through the story. Remember your characters' thoughts and feelings as well as actions.

Description is kept to a minimum. This will feature in the first draft.

The beginning of a sample story plan

Sarah and Rosie meet outside the gates of the fairground. The lights and noises are exciting and they pool their money – they only have enough for two rides each. They go on the dodgems and have a good time crashing into two older boys in their own dodgem. Sarah feels flushed as she climbs out of the car and she hears the two boys laugh as she and Rosie walk over to the ghost train. Will the boys come on the ride with them? Rosie jokes it might be nice to have the boys hold their hands when they're feeling scared. But when Sarah looks over her shoulder, the boys are wandering over towards the hotdog stand.

Feeling disappointed, she climbs into a waiting car and the ride jerks into action. She feels her smile fade as they plunge into the dark tunnel – she was secretly hoping the boys would join them. Still, the ride soon takes her mind off romantic woes. Strings of fake web get caught in their hair and unimpressive skeletons lunge out of coffins. This ride is a joke – it's not scary at all! But as they turn another corner the ride suddenly plunges and Sarah finds herself screaming with terror. She and Rosie are thrown free of the car into a stinking bog, with mud clinging to their limbs. Where are they? This isn't the fairground anymore!

Sarah pulls herself free of the mud and helps her hysterical friend climb onto dry ground. Two ghouls loom out of the fog and Sarah notices they look familiar – it's the older boys. But now their eyes are nothing more than dark shadows and their emaciated bodies are covered in bruises. They wear torn rags instead of their jeans and hoodies. One of them reaches out a bony hand to take Sarah's. She suddenly doesn't want to hold hands with that boy any more! She and Rosie run away, looking back over their shoulders to see the ghoul-boys

21 WRITING DIALOGUE

In novels for children, dialogue is probably the single most important element to master. It is where conflicts are dramatized, action takes place, the plot moves forward, and the characters are revealed. Dialogue is also the part of fiction that is closest to what it imitates. If you read it aloud, it takes only a little longer than the same conversation would take in real life. These qualities of realism and drama make dialogue central to fiction for children.

One author's story

The characters in children's author Meredith Sue Willis's novel *The Secret Super Powers of Marco* were based on children she taught in New York City. Outside of school, they cursed like drunken sailors and, in her novel, she included two curse words. One of the first things her editor told her was that the company had a policy against vulgar words in novels for children. Willis reports that her first reaction was to bristle: "That's how those kids talk!" Of course, her second reaction was that she wanted to see her book through to publication. She also noted that in real life, the kids actually cursed more than they did in her book. She had, in other words, already edited reality and was creating an illusion rather than simply transcribing. Also, she had to admit to herself that she didn't really want her eight-year-old son reading children's books full of language like that. In the end, she made her characters taunt each other with silly, invented insults like "Banana Brain!"

CAPTURING REALISM

Generally speaking, in order to capture the realistic quality of dialogue, your best strategy is to draft too much—too many quotidian and phatic exchanges, too many stage directions, even too many bits of description. Once you've captured the real-life quality to your own satisfaction, start cutting out everything but the very strongest parts.

STAGING

Dialogue in fiction is not simply a transcription of people talking. It also has to make crystal clear who is speaking with tags like "he said" when necessary. It must also give stage directions for how people speak using verbs and adverbs, as in "he snarled" or "he said angrily". It has to include some descriptions of gestures and actions. It may also include some narration, description of place or setting, description of the characters, and even a judicious amount of internal monologue.

WHAT TO INCLUDE

The operative word in writing dialogue in children's novels is "necessary." If the exchange is necessary, include it. If the description is necessary, keep it. If it is characteristic of Genevieve or necessary to the plot that she wears a floppy purple hat during the dialogue, by all means describe it. In fact, feel free as you draft your dialogue to describe her jeans and t-shirt as well, but in revising, be sure you get rid of the jeans and t-shirt if they don't help capture her character or advance the plot.

Be especially frugal with description and narration between lines of dialogue. You want as little as possible to slow the flow. "'I don't believe you!' she snarled" is better than "'I don't believe you!' she said, snarling in anger." The first example has fewer words and more momentum. Best of all, if it can be done without confusion, is simply "I don't believe you!"

TRY THIS

Below is a simple exchange of six words. Do anything you want to turn it into an interesting dialogue (combine speeches, add speeches, insert description, make it longer – anything at all).

> "Hi."
>
> "Hi."
>
> "Where were you?"
>
> "Nowhere."

Now take the six-word exchange and write another dialogue with it, this time making it a conflict between a teenage boy and an elderly lady. You may add anything you want, but include those six words. Notice in the example below how the teenager says very few words: he is sullen and withholding in this scene. The woman, however, blasts him with a lot of words. Whether people use many or few words is one of the important ways of showing the difference in their personalities.

> He ran down the hallway to her doorway and stopped. Her room smelled as bad as usual, sweet and musty.
> "Hi," he said.
>
> "Hi?" She shook a skinny finger at him. "Is that all you've got to say, you rude boy? I've been waiting for an hour! Your mother said you'd bring it directly! Where were you?"
>
> "Nowhere," he said glumly, holding out the oily, cold bag.
>
> She snatched it away and started gobbling the sandwiches.

> Janie was jumping up and down on the tree-house platform shouting "Hi! Hi! Where were you?" She was jumping so high, Frank was afraid she was going to crash through the boards.
>
> He hurried up the slope with his finger to his lip. "Nowhere special!" he shouted, and then, when he got close enough, he beckoned to her to lean down. He whispered, "Or maybe it was Very Special. Wait 'til you hear what I discovered!"

TRY THIS

Take a notebook to a place where there are a lot of children – a park, playground or schoolyard. Find an out-of-the-way spot, sit quietly, and transcribe what you hear. You'll quickly notice that you can't write fast enough to get everything down, but that's fine, because it means your brain has already begun to edit. Later, type up only the best of what you transcribed. Then – after you have the actual words spoken – reconstruct the other elements: what the kids looked like, where they were, how they said things. Make up what you aren't able to remember.

To extend the exercise, can you make your dialogue into a story? Might the scene be used in a story you've already started?

Next, take the same six words and use them in a story in which two friends have a mystery to solve. In this sample, the characters are both children, both full of energy, and speaking more or less in the same style. Notice, however, that what is going on in Frank's mind ("Frank was afraid...") gives him the quality of being a thoughtful, caring friend, whereas Janie seems impatient and perhaps reckless, based on the physical action ("She was jumping so high..."). The surrounding material in a dialogue (actions and thoughts) can go a long way towards developing and revealing character, too.

22 AVOIDING PATRONISING THE READER

Writing novels for children aged seven to 14 is more like writing for an adult audience than writing picture books. Your story will centre around characters who are children, and is probably shorter than a book for adults, but first and foremost it should be a good story about interesting people.

STARTING POINTS

You may begin with a situation or an issue in mind, but the essential rule in writing for children is to start with questions, not answers. If your theme, for example, is bullying, don't start with what you believe to be the best way for a child to deal with bullies. Rather, start off with a real person with a real problem. Approach your material as children approach life: without knowing how things will turn out. Children often don't even realize how things are supposed to come out, or that circumstances can change. The best novels for children are ones in which children simply deal with

Child's view
Keep in mind that a child's experience of the world is different from that of an adult.

life and life's challenges. The tone can be funny or serious; the tools the child uses to meet the challenges can be old-fashioned or modern, mundane or magical; but the way to be sure you are writing what children want to read is to write as if you were a child.

A CHILD'S POINT OF VIEW

This may sound obvious, but a writer for children needs to keep in mind that children see a special "slice" of the world. They are physically smaller than adults, and their senses tend to be sharper. They are experiencing many things for the first time, so their observations are especially intense. One way to move in this direction is to recreate some of your own memories as vividly as possible, using your senses in imagination: the odour of a schoolroom, for example, or the flavour of childhood sweets.

There are many ways to tell a story for children, but you may want to experiment with using first person or the close third person as a way of understanding the world as a child understands it. This doesn't mean the story has to be simple. You may put your child characters in any dilemma you please. The child may be pulled in

Physical difference
The fact that a child is smaller than an adult has a subtle effect on their perception of their environment.

The boy I imagine is dark, probably Latino, a small boy with a lot of hair that needs combing. He's all alone in a playground with some broken bottles. He's sitting in a swing. He swings a little, and then seems to decide that's for little kids and gets up and kicks at the broken glass... "I'm sick of being the big brother", he says. "All the time I have to watch my little sister! I'm telling you! She is so little but she's so much trouble! My mum has to work late and it's always me picking up my little sister from the babysitter and I have to make her peanut-butter crackers and she won't eat them if the peanut butter doesn't go all the way to the edges! I'm telling you. She gets to stay in the babysitter's house and watch television all day, but I have to go to school... school is okay, except for this big ugly boy Tyrone. Tyrone likes to pinch people. And you know what's worst of all? He lives on my block! And he wants to beat me up!"

One author's story

Meredith Sue Willis' first novel for children grew out of a little sketch about a boy who is feeling sorry for himself and starts committing acts of minor vandalism. He breaks off old-fashioned car antennas. In the story, he throws one car antenna into the air, and it turns magically into a star. It was just a scrap of an idea, but when Willis read it to friends, one said casually that she didn't think it worked, but that it might be interesting if told from the little boy's point of view. Willis tried revising it with the little boy telling "legends" about himself. How he got his star was one legend, how his little dog ran away was another, how he got a new friend another. And pretty soon, she had a whole group of linked stories that became her first novel for children.

TRY THIS

Pretending to be a child

Imagine the face of a child. This could be a child you have seen or an invented one, but it works best if it is not someone close to you. Visualize the face first, then where the child is: a specific place and a specific situation – an eight-year-old boy with dark hair that falls into his eyes, for example. He has just moved to a new neighbourhood. Now imagine that the boy begins to tell you about his life – he speaks very quietly, close to your ear: his mother is a single mum, his little sister likes to run away, he's worried about making new friends.

Move closer to him in your imagination, so that you slip inside the boy's head and hear his thoughts instead of his voice. He tells you how frightening the school bully is. He tells you a dream. He wants his own dog.

Next write as much of this as you can, not worrying about order or chronology. Just write in the child's voice. This exercise, by the way, is not meant to be an argument for using first person over third person, but rather a way to accumulate material and get to know the child. You might use some of the material in an internal monologue or even in spoken dialogue. It may also give you some ideas for your storyline.

Childhood memories

Think back to your own childhood for inspiration. Don't just consider the physical reality; how did you feel or respond in particular situations?

two (or more) directions. There may be shocks, betrayals; even death. But do keep in mind that the underlying worldview of a child begins with an acute sense of fairness and unfairness, and that children tend to persist in believing in a good outcome to the very end.

This is not to set up rules, but to suggest ways to enter into a child's experience. You may want to begin with your own childhood memories, or you may want to spend time observing children at play. You might also try that most childlike and enjoyable of all techniques: just pretend!

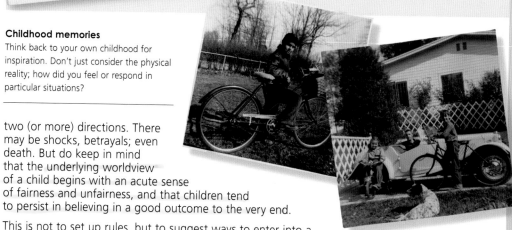

inside the mind of a child

Try putting yourself in his place to get a feel for your story.

23 THE WRITER'S VOICE

Who is telling your story? Is it you, the writer? Or is it the character? In Victorian times it was fashionable for the writer to be a palpable presence on the page, sometimes addressing their "dear reader" directly. Writers in this style would sometimes stop to make their own moral judgements about what was happening in their story.

Dialogue vs. narrative

It is vital in any story to get a good balance between dialogue – the bits of a story where the characters speak to each other – and narrative – the bits where the writer is describing something: the interior of the house, the view over the bay and so on. Readers are naturally drawn to dialogue. If they see paragraph after paragraph of narrative description they are liable to speed-read or skip them altogether.

THE MODERN WAY

Today, most writers would feel the intrusive approach only really works in an autobiography. The job of a fiction writer is to draw their reader into their story. As with film, television drama and theatre, you need to make the reader forget they are reading a book or watching actors on a stage or screen, and become utterly immersed in the story. The way to do this is to make yourself (as the writer) completely invisible.

MAINTAINING INTEREST

If you are writing with your character in the first person you need to adopt a tone of voice that the reader will find palatable or intriguing. No one wants to read 300 pages devoted to the thoughts of a carping middle-aged woman or a whining adolescent boy. Whether your central character is good or bad, the reader needs to be interested enough in them to want to carry on reading about them.

VERSION ONE: The band that they made

Dan came up with his Great Idea at lunchtime. It was the start of the autumn term. His friends were on the playing fields sitting among the fallen leaves under the big tree when Dan said, "Hey, who wants to be in a band?"

Dan had a myspace page and a battered Gibson guitar on which he could pick out three chords. Today he was wearing skinny jeans and a faded Ramones tour t-shirt. The t-shirt used to belong to his father, who was once featured on the front cover of *Rolling Stone* magazine under the banner headline, "He ROCKS." That was back in the eighties. Now Dan's dad drove a cab—when he hadn't forgotten to take his medication. Since Dan's mum left, there was no one to count out the little blue pills into the plastic cup.

Version one opens with a punch, taking the reader straight to the Great Idea. Details such as Dan's myspace profile and tour t-shirt bring the main character to life. Poignant revelations about family life – his mum's departure, his dad's reliance on pills – are mentioned almost as an aside, making them even more touching.

Show not tell

"Show not tell" is is one of the great rules of writing and one of the most difficult things to train yourself to do.

When you introduce a character don't tell the reader she is rich and beautiful. Say she arrived in a chauffeur-driven limousine and all the boys in the room could not keep their eyes off her. Don't tell your readers someone's mother is bossy or nosy; show her constantly interfering in the lives of her children or habitually asking searching and impertinent questions.

Showing rather than telling will make your characters come alive. They should appear as vivid, three-dimensional people to your reader, rather than cardboard cutouts.

CHARACTER BUILDING

Dialogue is where you are best able to "show" and not "tell" (see above). Is your antagonist unctuous and scheming? Show him flattering your hero and asking leading questions. Is he ill-tempered and prone to violence? Show him complaining about trivialities and threatening those around him with a beating.

Writing convincing dialogue is difficult. You need to ensure your characters are speaking with their own voice rather than yours. Reading your writing out aloud to yourself will help you polish your dialogue.

The version two sample indulges in "tell" rather than "show." The narrator tells the reader that Dan has been wearing the same t-shirt for three days, but it would be more entertaining to learn this by a description of the whiff!

Version two gets bogged down in detail. The reader learns Dan's age, his grade, the school's location and how old his sister is – all before getting to the meat of the story. Some of the language is detached and adult; this doesn't sound like the story of a young boy. The only piece of dialogue comes right at the end – from a secondary character.

VERSION TWO: The band that they made

Dan was thirteen and in year seven at Alderhay Middle School, which was just on the outskirts of a little town in Pittsburgh off Highway 32. It was lunchtime at the start of the autumn term. He'd always wanted to form a band. That morning, in between getting his sister, who was six, ready for school (their mother had left three years earlier) and measuring out his father's medication, Dan had mastered another guitar chord, bringing his repertoire to three. His father was a shambling casualty of the decade of the eighties and had spent the years in the hugely successful heavy rock band The Parasites. When he received an unusually large gratuity from a satisfied customer the Christmas before, Dan's father had acquired a Gibson guitar from ebay and then impatiently taught Dan to play the chords. "All you need is three chords, son", his father had said. "Just change the order of 'em and you can play anything."

Dan approached his friends (Steve Campbell, Big Phil Sane, Janey "Small Ears" Magoo, Little-Phil-so-as-not-to-confuse-him-with-the-other-Phil and Lou). They were sitting under the big tree, which is where they always sat, whatever the weather. Dan was wearing tight skinny jeans and a faded Ramones tour souvenir t-shirt two sizes too small for him. He'd been wearing that t-shirt for three days now. "Hey, I've had a Great Idea", he said. "Who wants to form a band?"

24 POINT OF VIEW

Although most stories have the same basic elements there are many ways to tell them. What you need to establish before you start the hard graft of writing is which angle you are going to take, and how this best serves the story.

YOUR CHARACTER'S AGE

If your main character is a 12-year-old boy, do you write "in the moment" or do you write from the point of view of an old man looking back on his life? As an old man you have the benefit of hindsight and wisdom. Perhaps, if your readers are older themselves, they will appreciate this point of view. But for writers of children's fiction, making the hero roughly the same age as your reader is generally far more effective.

Writing as an older character takes away an element of suspense – if your character is relating events that happened in the past, then they obviously survived those events. If you are writing as a 12-year-old caught up in dreadful circumstances, neither your character nor the reader has any idea what will happen next. Will the character survive the battle? Will he get lost in the woods? Will he drown in the shipwreck? Of course the character usually does survive – but the reader will not assume that if the story is written as it is happening.

Choosing the right tense

Some writers use the present tense to impart a sense of excitement. "We walk into the town. There's no-one around. Then I spot the flash of a rifle along a rooftop..." In the right hands this can be effective, but this breathless style can also be exhausting to read and difficult to maintain.

Most books are written in the past tense.

This can still sound immediate, especially if the writer uses terse and simple prose. "We walked into the town. There was no one around. Then I spotted the flash of a rifle along a rooftop..."

Be careful not to make your tenses too ponderous: "When we were walking into the town..." This will make your writing stodgy and slow the story down.

Five boy characters:

- *Stig of the Dump*
  by Clive King (1963)
  Stig is a caveman who lives at the bottom of a quarry. He's the person all boys would like to be: filthy, with no parents to tell him what to do and no bedtime.

- *Harry Potter*
  by JK Rowling (1997)
  Possibly the best-known hero of recent children's fiction. Seven fantasy novels watch Harry and his friends progress at Hogwarts School. Harry, an orphan, has a lightning-bolt shaped scar on his forehead. He's marked out in more ways than one – and he must learn to conquer the evil Voldemort.

- *James and the Giant Peach*
  by Roald Dahl (1961)
  Normal-boy James climbs inside a giant peach and, with his creepy-crawly companions, he takes readers on an adventure that defies belief.

- *Alex Rider*
  by Anthony Horowitz (2001)
  Alex Rider is often described as a young James Bond. This teenage boy is forced into working for MI6 after the death of his guardian. Mature and good-natured, Alex is a teenage spy readers like – and want to be.

- *Horrid Henry*
  by Francesca Simon and Tony Ross (1998)
  A series of books featuring a mischievous but likeable boy. Henry hates vegetables and homework – like a lot of other children.

Five girl characters:

- *Anne of Green Gables*
  by LM Montgomery (1908)

  An orphan character who has charmed generations of readers.

- *What Katy Did*
  by Susan Coolidge (1872)

  A mischievous girl who endears herself to the reader by being less than perfect.

- *The Worst Witch*
  by Jill Murphy (1974)

  Mildred tries hard at Miss Cackle's Academy, but often gets things wrong.

- *His Dark Materials* series (Lara)
  by Philip Pullman (first book of the series published 1995)

  A wild, tomboyish girl who learns to recognize the subtleties of good and evil.

- *I Capture the Castle* (Cassandra Mortmain)
  by Dodie Smith (1948)

  A witty heroine, living in a beautiful but crumbling house, faces the challenges of family and romance in the 1930s. Even modern teenage girls about to face adulthood can relate to her.

LOOK WHO'S TALKING

Most children's fiction writers choose to write in either the first person – "I" – or the third person – "he" or "she". In the third person you can still stick to telling your story entirely from one viewpoint, or you can vary your viewpoint by telling it from the point of view of other characters.

Writing in the first person gives your story an unbeatable immediacy. You have a direct connection to the hopes and fears of your main character that can make him or her seem to spring off the page. But, you are limited to telling the story from this one perspective. This can make depictions of epic events – such as a Napoleonic sea battle – quite a challenge. After all, when mighty warships – or even entire fleets – clash, you can only report what your character can see through the nearest gun port. So, seeing your story through the eyes of one character only can be quite restrictive.

A VARIED EYE

Writing in the third person – especially through the eyes of several characters – allows you variety. You can depict the action from whichever perspective will tell the story in the most exciting way. You can also give your reader an insight into the secret thoughts and motivations of other characters. You can tell your story from their point of view as well as that of your main character.

NARRATIVE PERSPECTIVE

First-person narrative: events can only happen as long as the narrating character is there to see them. The individual's "voice" influences the narrative tone.

I ran up the hill as fast as I could. I had to get away! I could feel my heart beating and the muscles in my legs pumping. When I reached the top, I looked over my shoulder. Oh no! The monster was still following me. I heard him give an almighty roar. There's no way I can outrun him, I thought.

Dan ran up the hill as fast as he could, desperate to get away. His heart was beating and legs pumping. The monster was hot on his heels. When he got to the top, Dan looked over his shoulder and saw that he was being followed. Dan heard the monster give an almighty roar and knew that there was no way he could outrun him.

Third-person narrative: The narrator can see and hear everything that's happening – even things the main character isn't aware of.

25 BEGINNINGS

You have your story mapped out, you're clear where you want to go and you've settled on your point of view and the age of your character. You're all ready to begin. So how do you draw your reader into the story and make sure they keep on reading?

START WITH A BANG

Do you start your story about Tom the farm-hand by giving an account of his morning visit to the cows, or do you start with "Tom could smell burning..."? Novice writers often make the mistake of opening their story by setting the scene: establishing the main character and the other characters around them, or painstakingly describing the house or village where they live. Even for historical fiction, where such detail is part of the intrinsic appeal of the genre, this is not a recipe for success. You need to grip your reader from the start and the best way to do this is with action and suspense.

PAGE-TURNING APPEAL

Action and excitement are essential ingredients in a story but nothing turns the pages better than mystery and suspense. After Tom has saved the barn from burning down he can come home to a note pinned to the kitchen table with a breadknife, saying "YOUR HOUSE IS NEXT". Then, as the story unfolds, the reader gradually gets to understand why Tom is in such a predicament, and wonders which of the other characters in the village is threatening him.

THE COMPETITION

Children have a bewildering array of distractions and entertainments. When it comes to filling their time, the proactive effort required to read a book faces stiff competition from such easy, passive pleasures as television, the internet, and computer games. Although your entire book should be exciting, the beginning must be unputdownable. After all, if your reader gets bored with it they're not going to make it to chapter two.

This is a poor opening paragraph because:

It opens with Rosie thinking about what she'd like to do. Thought is not the most exciting way of opening a story. It's an internal process, and one that only Rosie can have, with no action for the reader to become involved with.

Rosie's age is stated. Child readers tend to be aspirational – they want to read about characters older than them. If you say Rosie is eight, a nine-year-old reader might put the book down. Leave ages to the reader's imagination.

The reader is given several details about Mark, the younger brother. But who is the main character of the story? These details distract when we should be drawing our first sketch of Rosie – the person whose story we are about to hear.

There is too much literal detail about Rosie's actions. The reader doesn't need the minutiae of walking downstairs, through the kitchen, out of the door and into the yard. She can just race outside.

Eight-year-old Rosie thought about what she'd like to do today. Perhaps she'd go to the park, or perhaps she'd just stay at home. She went to find her brother, whose name was Mark and who liked to dig up worms in the backyard. He was two years younger than her. She was sure Mark would have a good idea about what to do. He always had good ideas. Rosie walked down the stairs and into the kitchen, then out of the back door and into the yard. Where was Mark?

GREAT OPENING LINES

❝There was boy called ustace Clarence crubb, and e almost eserved it.**❞**

C. S. Lewis, *The Voyage of the Dawn Treader* (1952)

❝It was a bright cold day in April, and the clocks were striking thirteen.**❞**

George Orwell, *Nineteen-Eighty Four* (1949)

❝It was the day my grandmother exploded.**❞**

Iain Banks, *The Crow Road* (1992)

Prologue 1:

Dear Reader

Welcome to a land far away. A young boy lives here – a boy without any parents. He has to find his own path in life, battling evil forces on the way. He will need your loyalty and courage as he encounters great evil. Will you stay by his side?

Prologues

Prologues are introductory paragraphs at the start of a story. They can supply a voice from outside of the story, introducing the world you are about to enter, or they can be a detail from the story you are about to hear, or they can work as notes from the narrator. The prologue works to whet the reader's appetite. It is often set in italic text to make it clear that it is not part of the main story.

The narrator's questions introduce the idea of choices within the story and paths not taken, and lead into the body of the narrative.

Prologue 2:

If I'd known then what I know now – would I have done the same things? Would I have stayed in the school dorms that night, safely tucked up in bed? Or would I have crept out of the latticed window and shimmied down the drainpipe all over again? I'll never know. But one thing I do know. Life throws up the most unexpected surprises—especially when you shimmy down a drainpipe...

This alternative is better because:

The book opens with a bang in the middle of the story – Rosie is already running outside.

It sets up physical details so that readers can imagine the characters: a pigtail bouncing; eyes shining with excitement.

The paragraph ends on a cliffhanger, drawing the reader in to keep on reading. What will Mark decide?

Rosie raced outside, her pigtail bouncing on her back.

"Mark!" she called up the garden. "Where are you?" Her little brother, covered in dirt, ran down the path towards her.

"What is it?" he asked. Rosie could see the excitement in his eyes.

"We're going on an adventure", she told him, holding out his backpack. She looked over her shoulder at the kitchen window, where she could see their mum clearing away the breakfast things. She hadn't noticed them.

"Where?" her brother asked, as Rosie turned back to face him.

She smiled. "You decide."

Instead of telling the reader that Mark likes digging in the backyard, the author shows him covered in dirt. The same detail is conveyed in both versions, but in version two the reader is shown rather than told.

Rather than describing Rosie's thoughts, the writer uses dialogue and action to propel the story: Rosie holds out a backpack to her brother and invites him on an adventure.

26 ENDINGS

A well-structured book will deliver a satisfying ending to make the reader feel all is well in the world and that the effort they have put into reading your book has been rewarded. A poor ending will leave them feeling frustrated and unlikely to want to read any more of your books. It is quite a responsibility to end your story well!

HAPPY ENDINGS?

It's a brave writer who ends his story with a dead main character. This might work in adult books or films (such as *Get Carter*), but it is an ill-advised ploy in children's fiction. Most parents, teachers and other guardians of your readers' morals will expect wrongs to be righted and good to triumph. This is the only "decent" thing to do. Besides, a reader who has cared enough about your main character to read your book from beginning to end will want and expect them to have a happy ending.

PLOTTING THE END

You need to ensure your story is paced correctly. You don't want the most exciting part of your novel to happen two-thirds of the way in and then slowly unwind to the end.

Here are two common conclusions in children's fiction:

➨ The wind-down: the book climaxes in the penultimate chapter – the hero survives a terrible battle, and the baddie is thwarted and apprehended. The final chapter could then have an elegiac, wistful flavour, where loose ends are tied up and your hero ponders on the lessons he's learned and makes peace with other characters. He looks to the future, full of hope.

➨ The surprise ending: something totally unexpected occurs to tie up the story and explain everything that has preceded it. (Also known as a "twist in the tale".) If you follow this approach successfully, your reader

GREAT CLOSING LINES

The pressure is off if you've brought your readers this far. Unlike opening lines, it's difficult to analyze why closing lines work, being so connected with the text that has gone before. Here are some iconic examples:

> ❝He loved Big Brother.❞

George Orwell,
Nineteen-Eighty Four (1949)

> ❝Thank goodness for that, he said, and handed him the tobacco jar.❞

J. R. R. Tolkien, *The Hobbit* (1937)

> ❝He would be in Jem's room all night, and he would be there when Jem waked up in the morning.❞

Harper Lee, *To Kill a Mockingbird* (1960)

will be gripped to the last, but you must ensure you have left sufficient clues and references in your previous chapters to make the revelation plausible.

BAD ENDINGS

If your reader has persevered with your book it is most likely because they have enjoyed the way you have written it. A bad ending will spoil the good work of the preceding pages.

Here are four pitfalls to avoid:

➡ The ending just tails off and the book ends with a whimper – did you get bored with your own story or find you were well over your word limit?

➡ Loose ends go unexplained – life is often like this, but people feel cheated if you don't explain how some key event earlier in the story came to pass.

➡ Hurried endings with glib explanations – readers want more for their time and money!

➡ Pointless endings – everything is the same as it was at the start and nothing has been resolved. Again, life is often like this, but your reader will expect something more satisfying.

LOOSE ENDS

A good ending should tidy all the loose ends in a story. Who was it that left that note that triggered the whole adventure back in chapter one? Who was the mysterious stranger who rescued your hero in chapter five? Beware though, of tying everything up too neatly, especially if you are thinking of doing a "What happened to them next" summary for your main characters. If your book is a success, your publisher – and your army of eager readers – will be crying out for a sequel. If you have already mapped out the future lives of your characters you will have painted yourself into a corner and have nowhere else to go.

THE OPEN-ENDED ENDING

The end of one book does not necessarily need to mark the end of your character or ideas. In series fiction, there are other ways to conclude a story:

Cliffhanger endings

Cliffhanger endings make it blatantly clear that the story is not complete. A hero who is literally dangling from a cliff, someone being kidnapped, a new romance appearing in the last pages – all of these will encourage the reader to stay with your characters beyond one book.

The subtle clue

The end of a story can leave clues to how another story might lead on. Is there one crucial mystery still to be solved? A missing character or parent your hero or heroine would love to meet? A baddie who has escaped justice? All of these details could lead into a second story.

Character development

In most stories, the reader likes to see the main character mature and learn something about themselves. By the end of one story, your main character may still have a lot to learn. He or she may have learned humility, but still might struggle with impatience. Could that impatience lead into a whole new story?

To be continued...

Three of the most enticing words in language. This old-fashioned but appealing promise to the reader whets any appetite. But make sure you can deliver. If you promise more stories, it is important to map out your series idea carefully.

27 AGE LEVEL

Children change so quickly as they grow up that their books must be carefully crafted to accommodate these changes. As children's understanding of language increases and they grow more confident in their ability to read, there are books to suit every stage of this development.

KNOW YOUR AUDIENCE

To write successfully for a particular age range, use your common sense. Anyone who has children or teaches them will have a head-start on a writer who is unfamiliar with the target reader. If you want to write for children, know your audience.

As your target age-level goes up, you can increase the length of your sentences and the complexity of your vocabulary. As a general rule, the younger the child, the shorter the sentences. Aim for sentences of fewer than 20 words. Avoid too many clauses, like the ones in this sentence, as they can be difficult to read and irritating to the reader.

SIMPLE DOESN'T MEAN DULL

Don't be afraid of invention and sophistication at any level. The successful *Voices in the Park* by Anthony Browne (Corgi Children's, 1999) uses a variety of inventive devices, and yet it's written for the kindergarten and elementary school level. It tells a simple tale – about a visit to the park – from the different perspectives of its four main characters. The artwork is extraordinarily vivid, borrowing from Symbolist and Surrealist painters, and the characters all have flaws and foibles. Yet the text is rarely more complicated than, "I felt really happy", or "I called his name". The end result is a deeply resonant book that *Publishers Weekly* described as a celebration of "the redeeming power of connecting with another human being".

Throw out the rule book

Especially when children share books with siblings and friends, reading ages can become blurred. The age distinctions help parents and teachers choose the right books for the right audience, but they should be used as a guide rather than a set of rules – for readers *and* writers.

TO LABEL OR NOT TO LABEL?

Some children's publishers place a colour-coded strip or a suggested age range on the spine or cover of their books. This enables teachers, or other adults buying a book as a gift, to have a clear idea of the level at which the book is pitched. But there is a down side to this practice. A struggling 10-year-old might find a book for six- to eight-year-olds more suited to his ability. But if it is labelled for this age-group, he might feel ashamed to be reading it and also lay himself open to mockery by his classmates.

HOW MANY WORDS?

There are some standard accepted lengths for children's books. Picture books rarely contain more than 500 to 600 words. "Early readers" for seven- to eight-year-olds will have around 1,000 to 6,000 words. Fiction pitched at older children could be anywhere between 30,000 and 60,000 words long. Any writer pitching a book to a publisher should bear these word counts in mind. If you go much beyond them, you will most likely struggle to get published.

MARATHON READS

Novels are invariably broken into chapters. Although you don't need to be consistent with chapter lengths, don't let them run too long. Most children will tire of a really long chapter. Plenty of short chapters will make a book more easily digested, especially for younger or less confident readers.

Broad levels

There are four broad age categories for children. Use the guidelines listed here to help you decide on the proper age range for your book.

AGE LEVELS

Reading ages are split into four broad levels. You will see books organized by these age ranges in bookstores. The word counts and page lengths detailed below are typical, but are not used exclusively; there is always some scope for flexibility:

0 to 3 years

Board books, cloth books, picture books; teaching the alphabet and simple words. These books will have no chapters and will rarely be more than 32 pages long.

4 to 7 years

As a child gets older, they turn to "first chapter books". This is the age at which children will first learn about a story being broken down into chapters, with a list of contents. A typical manuscript for this age-range will be about 4,000 words long. Books are often heavily illustrated and usually no longer than 64 pages.

8 to 12 years

Manuscripts in this age-range will be full-length novels of anywhere between 20,000 and 35,000 words long. A typical book will contain about 160 pages, with incidental illustrations.

13 years+

These books are aimed at the teenage market. Manuscripts can be around 60,000 words long and there is an increasing level of sophistication in terms of subject matter and narrative voice. Some of these books cross over into the adult market.

28 NOVELS

Children's novels cover the same genres as adult fiction – adventure, fantasy, horror, ghost stories and gritty social realism. Often it is only the lack of graphic sex and gratuitously sadistic violence that sets them apart.

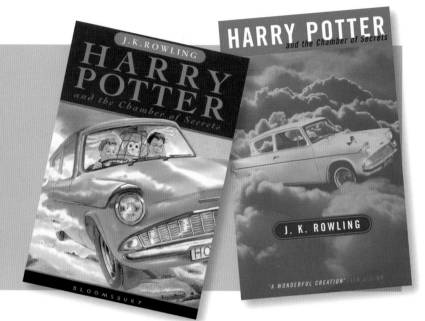

CROSSOVER BOOKS

Twenty-first century children's fiction seems to be going through a golden age – so much so that successful children's authors, such as JK Rowling, are often enjoyed by adult readers, too. This sub-genre of fiction has been described as "crossover". Rowling's UK publishers, Bloomsbury, even produce a separate edition of her Harry Potter series with a different cover, aimed at the adult market.

TWO STRANDS

Although publishers make micro-gradations between ages, pitching books at six- to seven-year-olds or nine- to ten-year-olds for example, children's novels fall into two main categories. First, there are stories for seven- and eight-year-olds often referred to as "first readers" or "primers". Such books are rarely longer than 6,000 words and are often part of a series or reading scheme. Then there are novels for older children. These will be considerably more demanding and run to 30,000 or 60,000 words. Pitching to exact ages here is more difficult. A confident eight-year-old may even enjoy books intended for a teenager or adult.

TABOO SUBJECTS

Some children's novelists, such as Judy Blume and Melvin Burgess, work successfully outside of the standard conventions of what is permissible in children's novels. They write about sex or drug use explicitly, for an early teen readership. While this approach has brought both critical and commercial success, most writers will find that raising these taboo subjects, and introducing swearing to dialogue, will make their books more difficult to sell – especially to schools, the home-school market and public libraries.

WHAT'S THE DIFFERENCE?

In its own way, children's fiction can be just as demanding and as sophisticated as adult fiction. Mal Peet's novel *Tamar* (Candlewick Press, 2007), for example, gained exceptional reviews. Set in the terrifying netherworld of the Dutch Resistance during the winter of 1944, it is a morally complex tale, unfolding across past and present, in which characters are referred to by several names. Moreover, many of the main characters are adults. The style and complexity of the story makes it an equally suitable read for adults and children.

Mad about the boy
Harry Potter has starred in seven novels that appeal to both child and adult audiences around the world, shown here with their British edition covers.

SOME BASIC RULES

As children's fiction is so varied, and children of all abilities will find their own level, it is difficult to make hard and fast recommendations. But aside from story length, there are a few general conventions that writers seeking to be published should stick to. Children's fiction almost always places children at the heart of the story. Also, the protagonist will usually be at the top of the age range or slightly older than your core readership. So, if you write a book for 10- to 12-year-olds, then your hero should probably be twelve or thirteen. Most children are reluctant to read about central characters who are younger than they are.

ADVENTURE

Stormbreaker
by Anthony Horowitz (2001)
The first in a series of books
following teenage spy, Alex Rider.

Artemis Fowl
by Eoin Colfer (2001)
These books may be set in a land of
fairies, but they are full of attitude.

All American Girl
by Meg Cabot (2002)
This book is full of adventure,
humor, and "Top Ten" lists.

Mortal Engines
by Philip Reeve (2004)
This futuristic adventure is
imaginative, epic and fast-moving.

Swallows and Amazons
by Arthur Ransome (1930)
Six children camp on an island in
England's Lake District.

FANTASY

Point Fantasy series,
various authors (1993)
A long-standing series of fantasy
stand-alone titles.

The Chronicles of Narnia
by CS Lewis (first book
published 1950)
Generations of children have had
their imagination fuelled by this.

Beast Quest series
by Adam Blade (2007)
This series makes reading exciting
for young boys.

Warriors
by Erin Hunter (first book
published 2004)
This series about wildcat clans has a
devoted fanbase.

Harry Potter series
by JK Rowling (first book
published 1997)
A seven-book series that has
changed the face of children's
book publishing forever.

HORROR

Point Horror series,
various authors (first book
published 1984)
A series of books that has kept
children reading after lights out.

The Midnight Library series
by Nick Shadow and
Damien Graves (first book
published 2005)
Each book is broken down into
three stories – ideal for short
attention spans.

Horowitz Horror
by Anthony Horowitz (1999)
Creepy short stories with a twist.

GHOST

Goosebumps series
by RL Stine (first book
published 1992)
This series satisfies readers who
want to come back again and again
for another dose of fear.

*Roald Dahl's Book of
Ghost Stories*
by Roald Dahl (1983)
Dahl did rigorous research
before compiling this collection
of fourteen stories.

Ghost Chamber
by Celia Rees (1997)
An ancient chamber and the restless
ghost of a knight templar.

SOCIAL REALISM

The Illustrated Mum
by Jacqueline Wilson (1999)
This novel teaches children that
no-one is perfect, not even parents.

*Angus, Thongs and Full-
Frontal Snogging*
by Louise Rennison (1999)
The first in a series of laugh-
out-loud books.

Doing It
by Melvin Burgess (2003)
This is a controversial and funny
novel for teenagers about sex.

WICKED

The pitfalls of slang

Writers who choose to portray the real world rather
than, say, fantasy or historical fiction, face the difficult task of
accurately reflecting how their characters speak. Children love slang,
and each generation has its own distinctive argot. Alas, nothing dates
like hipspeak, except perhaps for "cool" which seems to have survived
unscathed from the 1930s, when it first emerged from the American
jazz underworld.

Unless you're writing for naturally transient media such as comics or
teenage magazines, current slang should be used sparingly in fiction, if
at all. Children today may say "And I'm, like, soooo… whatever!" to
indicate indifference, and use "wicked" to mean good, but in 10 years'
time these mannerisms will seem as archaic and quaint as the 50s slang
spouted by hepcats and chicks in early Elvis movies.

Most people who write fiction from the heart rather than the wallet
will want their books to last. The more fashionable slang you use, the
more your book will date and it will have less appeal to future readers.

29 GRAPHIC NOVELS

Comics, in one form or another, have been popular with children of all ages since the beginning of the twentieth century. Hergé's *Tintin* books, for example, have a universal appeal and still sell well even though most were written more than 50 years ago. Although comics can be enjoyed by everyone, their combination of speech and illustration make them the perfect choice for reluctant or struggling readers. Over the last 20 years this form of storytelling has become increasingly more sophisticated, and the term "graphic novel" has been coined to describe comic books with genuine literary merit.

European genius

Created by Hergé (real name George Rémi), Tintin is recognized worldwide. One of the most popular characters from graphic novels, he's also probably the most long-running. The young reporter and his sidekick Snowy the dog first appeared in *Tintin in the Land of the Soviets*, published in 1930. Since then, many more adventures have been published, in more than 80 languages. Over 230 million copies of Tintin books have been sold worldwide.

WRITING GRAPHIC NOVELS

Unless they are without dialogue, such as Raymond Briggs' *The Snowman* or Quentin Blake's *Clown*, graphic novels have to be very tightly scripted. The writer must imagine their story in a series of boxes, like a movie storyboard. Most of the written information will be in the form of dialogue – in speech bubbles – with sparse narrative contained in boxes above or below the action.

SAME RULES, DIFFERENT STYLE

Graphic novels use the same rules of plot and character as any other fiction genre. The stories follow the same basic format of introduction, escalation and resolution; and characters and dialogue are as important as they would be in a conventional novel. Fans of the genre would argue that giving the story an added visual

Tex Ritter was a western star – one of the best-known "singing cowboys" of the 1930s and 1940s.

element enhances it immensely. Critics would say it takes the fun away from picturing these characters and their dramas in your own imagination. In fact, *The Old Classics Illustrated* series of comic books of 1950s and 1960s were literally books in comic format. Children's classics by Dickens, Jules Verne, H.G. Wells, and many more were simplified and adapted.

Rod Cameron was a film star in the 1940s and 1950s; he starred in Westerns among other things and was also immortalized in comic form.

Books in comic format
Here you can see a selection of comic books from the 1950s and 1960s – adapted and simplified from classic stories.

READ THIS!

For a perfect example of the creative use of comic formats in storytelling for younger readers look out for *It Was a Dark and Silly Night* edited by Art Spiegelman and Françoise Mouly (2004). Here, famous graphic novelists and illustrators such as Neil Gaiman, William Joyce and Gahan Wilson take this parody of one of literature's most infamous clichés and use it as a first line to build a story for seven- to nine-year-olds.

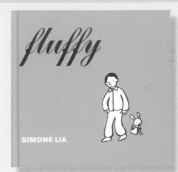

Fluffy

Fluffy, by Simone Lia is a fine example of a graphic novel for younger children.

DIFFERENT AUDIENCES

Many of the most popular graphic novels, such as Alan Moore's *Watchmen*, Frank Millar's *Batman: The Dark Knight Returns*, and Art Spiegelman's *Maus*, include levels of explicit sex, violence and real or imagined horror that make them unsuitable for pre-teen children. But this a broad genre. Comics such as *Flash Gordon* and *Superman* have become iconic figures of popular culture that appeal to both children and adults.

The classics
Many classic novels have made it into graphic format, along with characters from myth and legend, and figures of popular culture such as Superman (left) and Flash Gordon (below).

Renaissance man

British graphic novelist Raymond Briggs, writer and illustrator of classics such as *The Snowman* and *Fungus the Bogeyman*, likens his work to a film. As a writer and illustrator of graphic novels he is also:

- the director placing his characters in the frame
- the art director designing the sets
- the costume designer taking care that his actors' clothes are right for them and the period
- the cameraman, deciding whether to shoot the scene up close, or from a distance

The Journal of Luke Kirby

The Journal of Luke Kirby first appeared in *2000AD*, scripted by Alan McKenzie and drawn by John Ridgway. Luke is a primary school pupil who has discovered he has magical powers. Aided by his mentor Zeke, he fights against the evil that tries to infiltrate his hometown. Luke is roughly the same age as his readers – the comic has Disney-like vistas of the countryside that instantly establish a sense of time and place while creating a light-hearted atmosphere for the magical plot-lines.

Establishing time and place
In this early episode of *The Journal of Luke Kirby* the artist provides a wealth of background detail in the opening panel so that the reader has an immediate sense of time and place.

From strip to novel

Walt Kelly's "Pogo" the possum began life as a feature in *Animal Comics* in the late 1940s. When the cartoon became a regular strip in *The New York Star* its popularity soared – eventually, Pogo was signed by a syndicate and featured in four newspapers. Within five years, the possum was in over 400 papers in the United States. Kelly and his creation went from strength to strength – Pogo became the star of over 100 graphic novels, with around 30 million copies being sold worldwide.

Two consecutive dailies from Walt Kelly's Pogo strip. Note how Kelly uses the basic idea of Pogo's relationship to his son to provide several variations on a theme and milks the gag for all it is worth.

30 PAGE DYNAMICS

The design of a book is part of its message. A book with plenty of clean white space looks expensive, while bad typography makes a book look amateurish. This section introduces a few precepts of good book design in the areas of typography, grids and layouts; it demonstrates how to plan the visual pace and flow of the book; and finally, it offers advice on colour design.

TYPOGRAPHY

Fonts "say" something; they are not chosen at random. Although they exist in a different visual plane to the illustrations, we read meaning into the style of the typography as well as what is written. Children, before they can read, are aware of typographic conventions, and can see that typefaces can be expressive too.

FONTS

Fonts are broadly described as being "serif" or "sans serif". Traditional fonts like Times New Roman are serif fonts (defined as having a short decorative "foot" at the end of a stroke on a printed character); more modern fonts such as Arial and Helvetica are sans serif. Sans serif fonts are thought to be more legible for children learning to read. Fabula is quite a new font, developed after extensive research in the typographic department of Reading University in order to optimize legibility for young children. You can read about this font on their website at: www.reading.ac.uk/typography/research/typknowledgetransfer.asp

Three examples of traditional typefaces used in children's books.

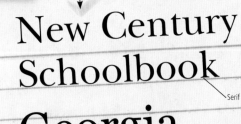

New Century Schoolbook — Serif

Georgia — Slab serif

Clarendon

Sense of calm
The delicacy of the artwork in pastel blue shades and the choice of font in the same blue sit comfortably together, evoking a sense of calm and mutual friendship.

Have you left space for the text in your compositions? Many illustrators fall into the trap of overlooking this important factor. Good typographic design is unobtrusive, and works in harmony with the artwork, whereas bad type will draw attention to itself and detract from the smooth telling of the story.

Ask yourself: will a child read this book to themselves or will an adult be reading it aloud? This is an important consideration when deciding on a typeface. Children have less familiarity with different letterforms, so very expressive type will be difficult to decipher for them. If an adult is reading the book to a small child, however, expressive type can be a fun part of the picture – and even onomatopoeic in some cases.

Integrated text and pictures

This example shows how text and images can be skilfully integrated to create exciting visual effects. There is a variety of text used, from designed fonts to hand lettering, which suits the style of drawing and the graphic collage and scanned computer images.

Artworked fonts

In John Lawrence's *This Little Chick* (Candlewick, 2002), the text and images work together, using an engraving print technique. Both image and text are balanced in weight, and the layout of the text reflects the meaning of the words. Most children's books are still designed with a serif or sans serif typeface. This is especially true if there is a lot of text to be read. Good book design relies on the text and images sitting comfortably together. Not all stories or media techniques suit hand-lettered or unusual typefaces.

CRASH COURSE

Stop Stealing Sheep and Find Out How Type Works
by Erik Spiekermann and
E. M. Ginger (1993)

Designage: The Art of the Decorative Sign
by Arnold Schwartzman (1998)

WEBSITES

Creating your own

Websites such as **www.fontographer.com** are an inexpensive way to create your own font. For a small fee, upload a template to generate your own hand-lettered alphabet, which is then scanned and sent back as a file. Now you can use the keyboard with your own font! Helpful websites include:

- **www.book-by-its-cover.com/**
  A blogger posts interesting book covers.

- **www.itcfonts.com/Ulc/4011/**
  An American typographic magazine.

- **www.eyemagazine.com**
  A graphic design magazine based in London.

TRY THIS

Text grids

Work to a grid when inserting text so that it conforms to a set of boundaries on the page, with controlled line lengths, and won't bunch up or fall into the middle of the page. Your illustrations can work around and through the grid, but the text should be in place before you think about the composition; there needs to be enough space and the artwork should not interfere with its legibility.

HAND-LETTERING AND COVERS

Hand-lettering is often used for cover artwork. The unevenness of the text stands out from the slickness of letterpress fonts and also creates a "cozy" feel suitable for children. Present it as a separate layer from the artwork to allow for foreign co-editions of your book to be created.

Remember that picture books will most likely be displayed with the cover facing outwards, but may be stacked with other books. Place the title in the top third of the composition. Avoid using all capital letters; this seems to SHOUT and intimidates a young reader. Book covers can be embossed, foil-blocked and have fabric and textural inlays.

Child's diary style
This book concept was based on a child's diary about her father needing and eventually having a heart transplant. The use of complementary colours enhances the simplicity.

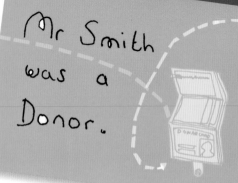

Integrating hand lettering
These three examples demonstrate further how hand lettering can be used to enhance and complement cover design.

Font categories

Decorative

- *Based on traditional metal type*

Fairgrounds, canal barges, pub signs and gravestone lettering, are all drawn from the folk art tradition. Illustrators' affinity with hand-lettering and ability to see words as images is part of this tradition.

Collage

- *Using a mixture of fonts together*

Kurt Schwitters, a 1920s Dadaist artist and graphic designer, created dynamic magazine layouts by using found lettering and defying layout conventions. He has influenced Neville Brody and Sara Fanelli.

Calligraphic

- *Fluid, "hand-drawn"*

In opposition to the restraints of holding a chisel or a nib pen (which create the serif of old-style fonts), holding a brush demands fluidity and spontaneity from the calligrapher.

Digital

- *Can incorporate everything*

Interestingly, digital font designers foreground the "drawn" elements of typographic design. No longer tied to a grid, they experiment with legibility and uneven point sizing.

31 PACE AND FLOW – STORYBOARDING

Storyboarding is an essential part of planning a picture book. Since imagery and text are symbiotic, storyboarding helps you work out the relationship between the two in rough form. Picture books are usually 32 pages long: 12 double-page spreads for the story with endpapers, title page and credits taking the remaining pages. Telling a story in 12 spreads is an art that requires you to tie the elements of pace, composition and colour together; storyboarding makes that possible.

CRASH COURSE

Illustrators who use composition in surprising and interesting ways:

Mr. Lunch Borrows a Canoe
by J. Otto Seibold (1994)

Biscuit Bear
by Mini Grey (2005)

A comprehensive and inspiring book about illustrating children's books:

Writing with Pictures
by Uri Shulevitz (1985)

Final composition
The storyboard is quite sketchy and is the perfect place to make notes and annotations about the story arc. However, note that the composition of the final spread artwork is almost unchanged; this is intrinsic to the working of the book as a whole and is fixed early on.

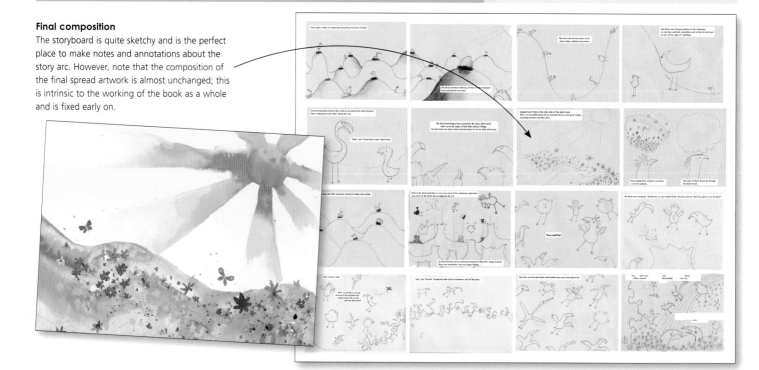

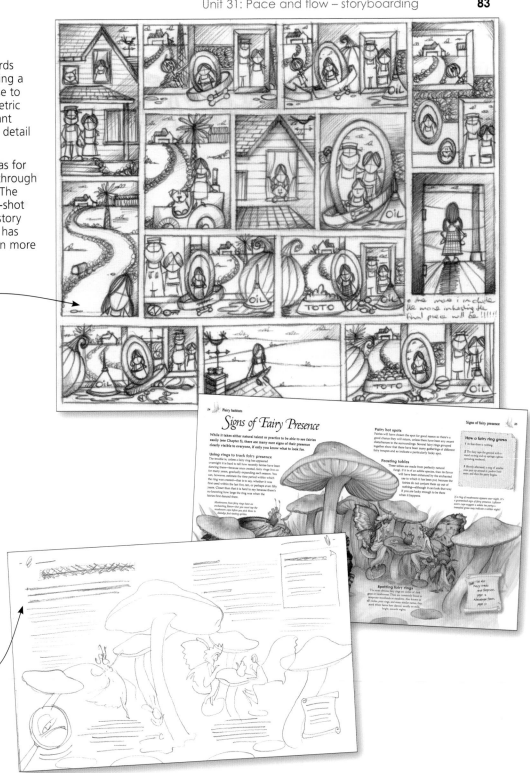

The varying approaches of these storyboards demonstrate the personal nature of planning a story at this stage. Some illustrators choose to work out the composition as rough geometric shapes; others prefer to block in a dominant colour. Some have a very clear idea of the detail in the imagery, even at such a small scale.

This set of work shows how the initial ideas for the book have been clarified and refined through constant reworking and problem-solving. The drawings show a variety of close-up, long-shot and dynamic compositions that keep the story interesting for a young reader. The colour has been thoughtout too, which is explained in more detail further on in this section.

The book in miniature
Here, the storyboard represents the vision of the finished book in great detail. Nearly every element that will finally appear on the pages is here.

- It gives you a "bird's-eye" overview of the narrative.
- It helps you pace the story.
- You can try out different strategies to create visual movement.
- It helps you to check the rhythm of the story and find similarities and anomalies in the page compositions.

Text weights
On a slightly larger scale, you can use the storyboard technique to plan "thumbnails" of spreads, showing where images will be placed and the distribution of text weights. This technique is often used in non-fiction.

TRY THIS

- Draw up a set of 15 spreads on a large sheet of paper, blocking out the first two and the last one. This leaves you with 12 spreads to tell your story. Using layers of layout paper, work out your story quickly in thumbnail form. There is no need for a lot of detail. When you have finished, lay another piece of paper over the first one and work out the story in a little more detail. Now show your work to someone else – can they make sense of the story from your drawings? Is the emphasis of the story in the right place? Have you left room for the text in the compositions? Have you made sure that nothing important is in the gutter? When you come to do the "finished" artwork, you can enlarge these tiny sketches and use them for reference to keep the scale and freshness of your initial ideas.

- Take a picture book with compositions that you admire. Using the same grid as before, thumbnail the compositions in terms of simple geometric shapes and colours. This is a useful way to visually analyze a book's design. You can use the basic layouts and pictorial strategies as a starting point for your own compositions.

Nicole Tadgell uses a storyboard to work out the visual pace and flow of a story called *Fatuma's New Cloth* by Leslie Bulion (Moon Mountain Publishing). She plans her storyboards as film directors plan movies, so the first two images are "zoomed out", showing the landscape of Tanzania where the story takes place. Then we gradually "zoom in" and see the two main characters and become involved in their story. The illustrator keeps the action interesting, varying the sizes of the characters from close up to farther away, and even crossing the gutter for more dramatic effect.

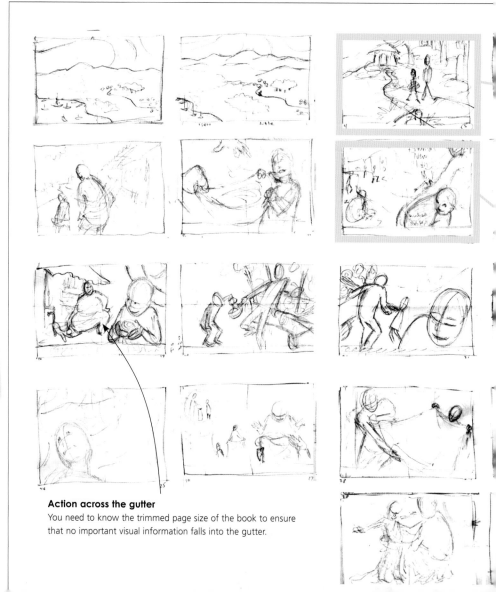

Action across the gutter
You need to know the trimmed page size of the book to ensure that no important visual information falls into the gutter.

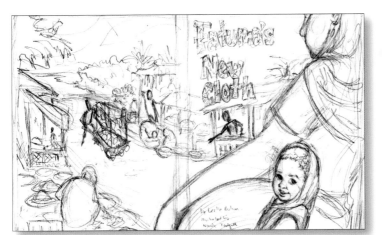

1 Jacket rough
Pencil rough of jacket image with type roughed in, and more final watercolour image. The cover was commissioned to be done first, so the publisher could make catalogues and other promotional materials.

"I am glad to have your help in the market today, Fatuma."

"I like to carry the basket for you, Mama."

2 Watercolour test
This is a "colour test" created on low-quality paper. It's actually a photocopy of the final drawing, painted very loosely and quickly because the illustrator's goal was about making colour choices for the whole book. Since both characters were side-by-side on this page, it was good to make sure their kanga cloth colours went well together.

3 Final illustration
This is the final jacket illustration. It's watercolour paint on watercolour paper. The composition, surprisingly, did not change at all from the initial sketch (top) to the final image.

VISUAL STORYTELLING

These spreads from *Pudding* by
Pippa Goodhart and Caroline Jayne
Church (2004) show the variety of
composition and "film language"
employed in telling a story visually.

1 *The characters are shown on different sides of the
double page spread, in the same pictorial plane but
separated by the gutter.*

2 *The horizon line moves up and pushes the protagonists to
the back of the picture plane. In the foreground, other
children and other puppies are playing, to underline the
message that the girl and the dog should be friends.*

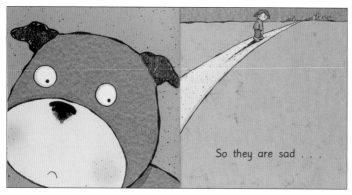

3 *The use of extreme close-up on the dog is a good way to show heightened
emotion in a character as it allows you to draw their expression in greater detail.
The "long shot" on the girl gives us a sense of her isolation. She is walking away from
the dog – this leads the reader into the next page, as we read from left to right.
Characters usually move in this direction unless the story is making a point.*

4 *The horizon line of the floor leads the eye up the side of the tablecloth and down
the spilt milk to where the dog is hiding.*

5 *The curved diagonal creates a springing dynamic to this composition, adding
movement to Pudding's escape.*

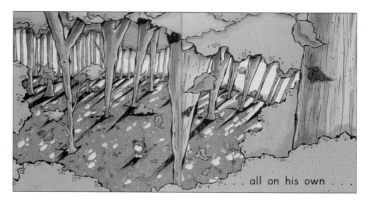

6 *The forest is a mass of vertical lines: the forced perspective gives a bird's-eye
view of this part of the story. The dog is hard to find, and a sharp-eyed child
will see that he is not alone, as the text suggests, but that the little girl is hiding
behind a tree nearby.*

7 *The girl reaches over from the right-hand page to stroke the dog on the left-hand page. This breaches the visual distance that they had before.*

8 *The two characters find each other but are still separated by the gutter and are on different horizon lines. They have made eye contact.*

9 *Extreme close-up of the two characters together reinforces that this is the emotional core of the book – the point of the story.*

10 *The characters revisit the scene of Pudding's earlier misery and run back down towards his home, away from the woods where they both were lost.*

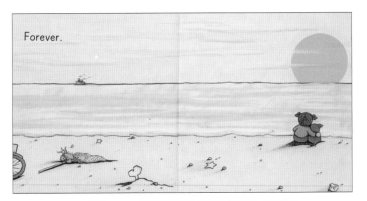

11 *The characters are together on an adventure, almost moving out of frame at the side of the book.*

12 *The stable horizon lines emphasize the new-found security of the friends. They are shown with their backs to the reader in a medium long shot as the "camera" disengages from the story.*

32 DUMMY BOOKS

Creating storyboards and rough mock-ups of your book will have allowed you to plan and explore its structure, but to get a real sense of the finished product you need to create a much more accurate "dummy" version. You can use this to convince a publisher that your book is a product worth publishing. The finished dummy should look as similar to the intended end result as possible in terms of format, content and feel.

ASSESSING YOUR BOOK

This is the point at which you make up pages of the intended size, or format, of the printed book. You may find that what works on a small scale does not work compositionally on a larger scale. Pin your double page spreads sequentially on a wall or lay them out on a table and look at them critically to see if the pace, flow, feel and structure of the book is exactly as you want. Make changes at this stage if you need to.

Once you are satisfied with all the spreads, make accurate detailed line drawings of the pages, blocking the text as accurately as possible in terms of style, point-size and the space it occupies on the page, whether it is hand-lettered or a font. Photocopy or scan the double page spreads, and use these copies to make up the dummy book.

You can also produce a more detailed dummy by creating final pieces of artwork for two or three spreads. Use the finished artwork to show your media and technique skills. Photocopy or scan them and integrate these copies with the other detailed line drawing pages. See page 138 for more about making dummy books.

Dummy book example

A dummy book lets the illustrator see how the artwork works dynamically across the spreads, and whether any vital information will be lost in the gutter.

Spread overview

Printing or sketching the spreads that make up a book as small "thumbnails" allows you to see how the imagery in the book works as a whole, and to get a sense of the pacing.

COMPOSITION TIPS

It is often possible to reduce strong page designs into their basic component elements in order to analyze how and why they work to engage the reader and enhance the narrative.

- Contrasting simplicity and lots of white space on some pages with full, complex images on others adds variety and interest.

- Playing with scale can make page layouts more dynamic.

The duckling is standing in a field of simple vertical lines of foliage, looking up at the swans flying in horizontal lines across the top of the page, creating a sense of calm, order and balance (above and right).

The combination of the hen in the top left corner, the little chick in the middle and the smaller hen in the bottom right corner creates a sense of movement along this diagonal composition, which is increased by the exaggerated actions of the characters (below and left).

Showing only one leg and part of the body exaggerates the elephant's size and weight. Placing the image in a white space draws attention to the hedgehog straining under the weight of the elephant.

The figure in the foreground is cropped very severely, which forces the reader to engage with the character.

"When I was a boy, I wanted a dog," said Grandpap. "You're going to wish for a dog."
Charlie shook his head.

WRAP-AROUND COVER

Many hardback books have a simple, loose, wrap-around cover or dust-jacket. Usually the book binding is plain with the cover design appearing only on the dust-jacket itself. Remember to allow for the width of the cover boards of your book in any measurements you make so that the cover fits exactly. For more on making a dummy book, see page 138.

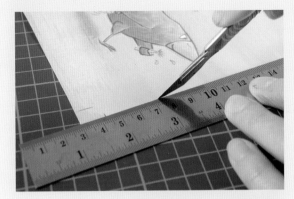

Prepare the artwork
Prepare the artwork including the necessary extra measurements around the edges. Trim the height of the cover along the registration marks, to fit the height of the cover of the book.

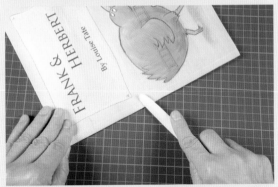

Form the spine
Measure the spine and mark the measurement on the cover illustration. Fold and press the width of the spine on the cover illustration using a bone folder.

Cover the book
Place the book into the folded space and fold the ends around the edges of the book. Press down firmly with a bone folder. Place the loose cover around the book.

33 COLOUR THEORY

The ever-expanding range of colours available across a wide range of media can be a little overwhelming. It is important to understand how colour works and how to mix colours in order to produce a successful and professional-looking piece of final artwork.

LEARNING COLOUR CONTROL

Studying the theory behind colour combinations will enable you to develop the same level of control over colour as you have over the composition of an illustration. Investigate colour mixing and colour combinations, and explore how you can vary shades and tones to create weight, depth or atmosphere. Learn by critically assessing how other successful illustrators control their palettes. Take inspiration from nature and all forms of art and crafts. Spending time on basic colour exercises may seem laborious, but it is well worth the effort. The colour wheel shows some simple but very important colour theory principles that you can use to make your work stronger and more characterful. It does not have to be followed slavishly, but understanding a few simple guidelines will benefit you greatly.

THE COLOUR WHEEL

When the primary and secondary colours are arranged in a circle they form a "colour wheel". Primary colours are red, yellow and blue. In theory you can mix any colour from just these three. Browns and neutrals can be mixed from combinations of the three primary colours. The secondary colours are created by mixing two primaries in equal or varying amounts.

WARM AND COOL COLOURS

Cool colours are usually thought to be green, blue and violet, and warm colours thought to be red, yellow and orange. In simple terms, they can be used to create the illusion of space and depth; cool colours appear to recede and warm colours seem to come out towards you. Apply cool colours for the backgrounds and warm colours for characters or foreground objects.

Six-section colour wheel
A basic colour wheel shows the primaries and secondaries. The former can only be bought as manufactured pigments, and the latter can either be bought or mixed from the neighboring primaries.

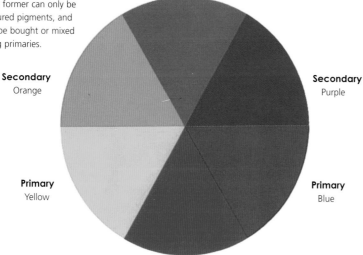

Primary
Red

Secondary
Orange

Secondary
Purple

Primary
Yellow

Primary
Blue

Secondary
Green

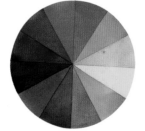

Tertiary colour wheel
Mixing the primaries and secondaries on the basic wheel gives six extra mixes, or colours, called "tertiaries".

Two halves
The wheel can be roughly split in half to show warm and cool segments.

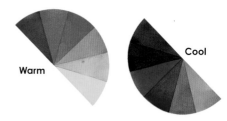

Warm

Cool

Each pigment has its own warm or cool bias. For example, cadmium yellow has a lot of red in it, making it warm, while lemon yellow has a cool blue bias. Keep this principle in mind as you mix clear bright secondaries that aren't dull or muddy. We have seen in the colour wheel opposite that red and blue make violet, but which red and which blue? Is it cadmium red or alizarin crimson? And is the blue colour cobalt, phthalo or cerulean?

HARMONIOUS COLOURS

This colour scheme, also known as "analogous colours", uses hues that lie next to each other on the colour wheel; for example, shades of green, turquoise and blue are harmonious. It is an easy way to be sure that your colours will work well together, although the scheme may lack a central focus or punch.

COMPLEMENTARY COLOURS

"Complementary" can be a confusing term when it is used to describe the relationship between colours, because it refers to the colours that lie opposite each other on the colour wheel. When put together they seem to dance or vibrate, as in some of Bridget Riley's paintings of the 1960s. This principle can be used to shocking visual effect in your illustrations. For example, if you wanted a lively colour scheme, you could use red and green as the main colours. Adding a black outline helps to retain shapes of characters and objects against the background.

Cool

"Cool" blue   "Cool" yellow   "Cool" red

Warm

"Warm" blue   "Warm" yellow   "Warm" red

Colour bias
The colour bias of a pigment shows up clearly when it is placed next to a similar hue (right). The choice of primary colour determines the resulting secondary mix. Those closest together on the wheel create intense secondaries (below left), while those farthest apart create more muted secondaries (below right).

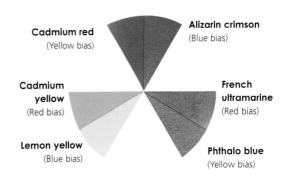

Cadmium red
(Yellow bias)

Alizarin crimson
(Blue bias)

Cadmium yellow
(Red bias)

French ultramarine
(Red bias)

Lemon yellow
(Blue bias)

Phthalo blue
(Yellow bias)

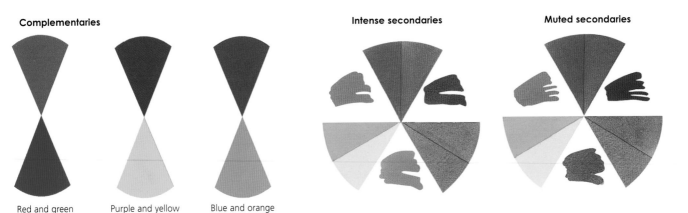

Complementaries

Red and green   Purple and yellow   Blue and orange

Intense secondaries

Muted secondaries

TRY THESE

Art materials can be expensive, so it makes financial and aesthetic sense to try some colour exercises to know what works best for your illustration.

Use the exercises shown here. If you purchase a new colour it is a good idea to test it with your favourite colours to see how the two colours combine. The results might surprise you.

Flame red   Winsor green

Alizarin crimson   Winsor green

Neutrals test
Mix the complementary colours red and green. See how the blue-biased alizarin crimson adds a more violet tinge to the neutral mix.

White-out test
Test colours in progressively whiter mixes to make lighter tones. Note – it doesn't take as many steps to create the lighter-toned yellow.

Colour match test
Paint or shade with pencil your own greyscale in nine or ten graded steps. Then try mixing a colour into swatches to match the scale. Here ultramarine has been mixed with black and white to make a shade and a tint respectively. However, it is best to avoid adding black to a colour in an illustration as it can make the colour dull.

NEUTRALS

Not all your work will require bright colours; sometimes a muted or subtle colour scheme is appropriate. Rather than use manufactured greys or neutrals you can mix your own using complementary colours. We have already learned that if they are used as pure pigments set by each other, complementary colours set up a vibrant contrast. When physically mixed, however, they create a neutral grey. The better the visual complement (i.e. the better the position of the two colours opposite each other on the colour wheel), the more neutral or unbiased the resulting grey. Experiment with different complementary mixes and see which you prefer.

Mixing grey
The complementaries emerald green and cadmium red mix to make a subtle yet characterful grey neutral.

TONE OF COLOURS

This is the degree of lightness or darkness of a colour. Each colour has its own tone in its pure, unmixed form. The tone of yellow is fundamentally lighter than blue when compared to a greyscale. But you can change this by adding a lot of white to the blue to make it lighter in tone, or by adding ultramarine to yellow to make a rich dark green. So why is this important? Assessing the tones of your work as you go helps you emphasize the elements you want so they have a more dominant tone than the rest of the illustration. Try half-closing your eyes (it simplifies the details so you see the tones more clearly) or looking at your work in a mirror. This way you can assess the range and hierarchy of tones in your visual story.

A blue mixed with white to make a lighter tone – this is known as a tint.

A green mixed with black to make a darker tone – this is known as a shade.

The important secondary

As the main colour in nature, green is the most mixed of the secondaries. It can be a difficult colour to paint with – many of the most successful greens are mixed from two primary colours (blue and yellow) rather than applied directly from a green pigment. Luckily there is a large range of cool and warm blues and yellows, so the possibilities for creating shades such as lime and moss are vast. To begin, acquire a selection of yellows and blues (as well as black) to give you a variety of options for green shades. Not only will your particular shade be more unique, but it's fun to do. You can also modify a bought pigment green to make more varied shades. Then try the deceptively simple exercise as shown here.

Blue and yellow don't necessarily make green

This is another fun exercise to try. Make a chart by mixing a selection of six or so blues and yellows. Choose colours that will exemplify the full range of possibilities – for example an orangey yellow and a turquoise – so that you discover the subtle brown greens and emeralds that are possible. Keep the chart pinned to your wall for reference, and remember to make notes of the colours. In six months you will have forgotten!

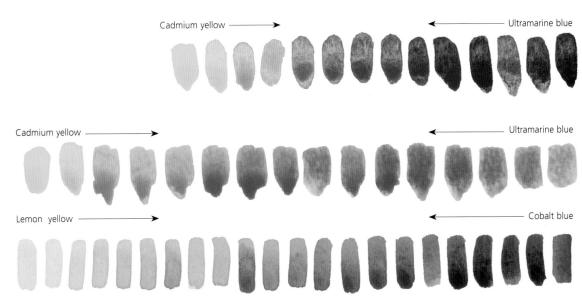

Cadmium yellow ⟶   ⟵ Ultramarine blue

Cadmium yellow ⟶   ⟵ Ultramarine blue

Lemon yellow ⟶   ⟵ Cobalt blue

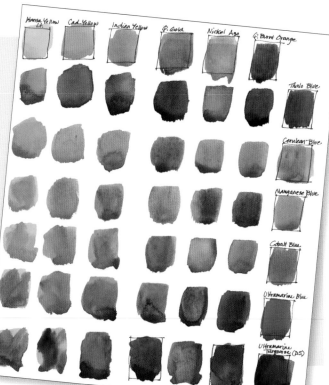

CRASH COURSE

Colour Harmony 2: A Guide to Creative Colour Combinations
by B.M. Whelan (1995)

The Complete Colour Harmony: Expert Colour Information for Professional Colour Results
by T. Sotton and B.M. Whelan (2004)

Watercolour Mixing Directory
by Moira Clinch and David Webb (2006)

34 DESIGNING WITH COLOUR

Colour is an important tool that an artist can use to communicate. In picture books, where the visual impact of illustrations is fundamental, colour can have a considerable influence on how a story will be read if it is used carefully.

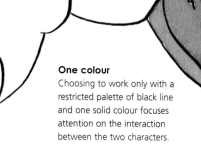

One colour
Choosing to work only with a restricted palette of black line and one solid colour focuses attention on the interaction between the two characters.

Limited palette
A limited palette of colours, using subtle, dark hues, heightens the story's mood, in which the boundaries between dream and reality are blurred.

COLOUR PSYCHOLOGY

Colour enhances the mood and atmosphere of a story. Not only does each colour have its own particular associations, but the colour in an illustration often communicates the story's tone before words are read. Colours in picture books need not be realistic or true to life. For example, trees may be blue or pink, dogs red or elephants multicoloured (think of Elmer). The important thing is that the child recognizes and identifies the images and shapes.

Two colours
The use of flat colour as a background focuses attention on the detailed line drawing and creates a contrast between the two. The addition of a small area of a second colour directs the eye to the focal point on the page – the sleeping duck.

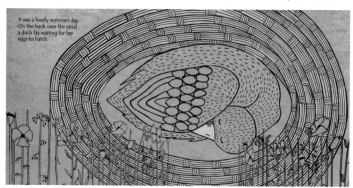

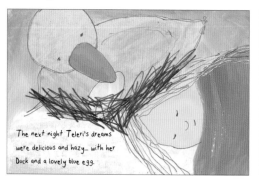

Your choice of colour may be dictated by the story – for example it might be set at night or on a hot, sunny day. Sometimes a limited, or even monochrome, palette is used for reasons of fashion, simplicity or to emphasize a character in a story where the situation is immaterial. Whatever the reason for your choices, they should be well considered to strengthen the impact and intention of the book.

yellow thing in the garden.

Experiment
Paint a different colour option for a central image such as a frog, then try various colours of backgrounds and see how the harmonious colours act as a camouflage while the stong complimentary or tonal contrasts exaggerate the shape or surreal nature of the image.

Pure colour
Using primary and secondary colours gives a bright, colourful feel for younger children. Focus on the main character has been achieved by using black for Patch the dog, which creates contrast and makes him stand out from the colourful backgrounds.

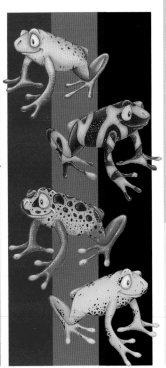

READ THIS
Pumpkin Soup
by Helen Cooper (1998)

Moody, atmospheric and use of limited palette.

Don't let the Pigeon Drive the Bus
by Mo Willens (2003)

Contemporary feel to a simple, humorous story.

Princesses oubliées ou inconnues (the Princesses Series)
by Rebecca Dautremer (2004)

A French illustrator uses red and green with sophistication.

Farmer Duck
by Helen Oxenbury (1992)

Realistic representation of the weather, time of day and situation.

CRASH COURSE

Designer's Guide to Colour: Bk. 5
by I. Shibukawa and Y. Takahashi (1992)

Looks at combinations of colours to suggest palettes for different psychological needs.

35 PAPER ENGINEERING

Although often classed within novelty books, the tradition of "true" pop-ups (three-dimensional structures formed by creasing paper and activated using kinetic energy) is essentially paper construction based on three simple formulas: the "V" fold, the parallelogram and the "45" fold.

PAPER ENGINEERING

An artist who creates pop-ups is known as a "paper engineer". Most paper engineers learn their craft by dismantling existing examples, but there is an increasing number of instructional books that explain the basic mechanics. Learning the rules will give you a sound basis and understanding to work from. But once learned, the rules are there to be broken!

The production of a pop-up book is a carefully planned process. During the design process you will need to play with many paper samples to resolve the mechanics. Most often the paper engineer only plans the mechanics and employs an illustrator to create the visual effects.

Pop-ups can be very simple or sophisticated, depending on the target audience they wish to engage, the story or concept and the budget of the publishing house. The only limitations are those of the imagination of the designer!

Pop-ups for young readers
Paper-engineered books can be great fun for young children. But remember that they will need to be robustly designed and free of sharp corners.

TRY THIS

Making a pop-up

The simplest pop-up construction is the "V" fold. It requires only one folded pop-up piece with gluing tabs and gives you the opportunity to see how size and angles will affect the projection and the composition on the page. It may be simple but it still requires accuracy of folding, cutting and gluing if the pop-up is to sit comfortably within the double page spread.

Materials you will need:
- Paper or card (149 lb)
- Pencil
- Steel ruler
- Craft knife (with a new blade)
- Scissors (with a sharp point)
- Scoring tool – such as a dry ballpoint pen
- Glue – clear, solvent-based (not a glue stick)
- Cutting mat
- Paper knife – to stick down corners and edges and ensure accurate contact

Method:
1 The book is designed by the paper engineer and tested as a rough dummy. Tracings are used for nesting (determining how much paper will be required) and can also be used as a guide for creating the artwork. Minor changes are often made before the die is planned and artwork produced. A working dummy is produced from the first proofs and the operation of the pop-up tested before investment is placed in the mantling of the final die to cut the paper.

Pop-ups are printed and then assembled by hand as a labour-intensive process usually carried out abroad.

2 There are three kinds of folded line in a pop-up mechanism: valley folds (crease goes back from view); mountain folds (crease comes forwards towards you); the spine of the book (centre of the double page, base to the mechanism). Remember to score all the folds with a ruler and scoring tool to ensure they are straight and crisp.

Arts and crafts
Paper engineering takes beautiful illustrations and artefacts to another level in high-specification books.

Pop-up non-fiction
Pop-ups can be a fabulous way of bringing concepts to life in a very tangible and understandable way for all age levels, making them the perfect medium for highly illustrated non-fiction.

Looking through
Paper engineering can be as simple as an extra fold-out page with a die-cut hole. This provides another layer of possible interaction and interest for the reader.

CRASH COURSE

The Elements of Pop-Up
by David A. Carter and James Diaz (1999)

An excellent range of samples to unpick and put back together.

The Pop-Up Book
by Paul Jackson (1994)

Simple diagrams, clear explanations and photographed samples illustrate the professionalism of the craft.

Pop-Up: A Manual of Paper Mechanisms
by Duncan Birmingham (1999)

This book offers clear step-by-step instructions and drawings.

Paper Engineering for Pop-Up Books and Cards
by Mark Hiner (1986)

Read this book to gain a more thorough understanding of pop-up book mechanics.

36 NOVELTY BOOKS

Novelty books are designed to appeal to the curiosity of young children and promote learning through play. Investigation using touch, pull tabs, turning wheels, lifting flaps and mirrors has inspired and generated a diverse range of published material.

CRASH COURSE

The Very Hungry Caterpillar
by Eric Carle (first published 1969)

This is possibly the most popular novelty book of all time. It is based on a simple storyline, but the overall design of the book is what makes it really special. The use of texture, colour, and white space stimulates intrigue and makes it a delightful book for children.

Dear Zoo
by Rod Campbell (1982)

Very simple, this book delights children as they uncover the animals from page to page.

Peepo
by Alan and Janet Ahlberg (1983)

Slightly more sophisticated, this book is comprised of a series of holes that peep through to the next page. It has lots of interesting elements to reveal!

Pop-out scare
Haunted House by Jan Pieńkowski is a pop-up book full of shocking surprises and creepy scares. As readers enter the rooms page by page, imaginatively designed creatures jump out from hidden corners.

I can't seem to settle down.

"Shiver me timbers," he said. "I see a pig in the sky!"

helicopter

Interactivity
Pirate Pete by Nick Sharratt introduces an element of interactivity by using cut-out "stickers" that can be inserted in slots to complete sentences.

seagull

crown

doughnut

crocodile

spaceship

Novelty books can be produced with a wide range of materials. Padded, textured or cutaway book covers enhance the look of a book, and gimmicks such as plastic squeaky toys are used to attract attention. Microchip technology offers the use of unlimited everyday sounds, play tunes, and nursery rhymes and it is also popular for books to include small gifts or CDs. The publishing market is competitive and has to respond to the needs of consumers wanting more for their money than just a book!

COMPETITION FOR LEISURE TIME

An increased disposable income of many families, huge technological developments and changes in the use of leisure time has put tremendous pressure on the traditional pastime of reading. The vast range of entertainment available to the more fortunate and demanding generation of today means that concepts in children's publishing need to be original and eye-catching if they are to compete and survive.

Books or toys?
Increasingly sophisticated production techniques and the resulting lower cost of producing novelty books has led to an explosion of products that blur the line between simple reading material and interactive toys.

TRY THIS

Design some spreads

Using the theme of "Jungle Animals", design five double-page spreads to visually stimulate a young child. Experiment with collage and three-dimensional materials, be imaginative and remember: if images are produced three-dimensionally, they need to be photographed to indicate how the final artwork would be seen.

Make a board book

Generally, a board book or pop-up book contains six to eight pages, although they can sometimes have 12 to 16. The process of putting together a mock-up board book is the same as a picture book, but uses sheets of stiff card cut accurately to the correct page size, and placed between the photocopied pages.

TIP

Textures and foils can look professional enough in mock-ups – if glued very carefully – but the extra weight will make it more likely to pull apart, so use the appropriate glues. Avoid getting glue on the pages and artwork – mock-ups still need to look clean.

37 BOOK JACKETS

The book's cover, or jacket, not only protects its pages but is a major selling point in the very competitive market of children's books. The marketing of a book relies on the jacket for its success.

MAKING COVERS WORK

Most children's books have illustrated covers, sometimes fully illustrated, and sometimes partly illustrated. A good book jacket reflects the style and content of the book in a way that captures the attention of a potential buyer. To ensure that this requirement is met, there is often a close working relationship between the designer and illustrator, editor and marketing department within the publishing house.

TIPS FOR JACKET DESIGN

Be aware that a picture book will most likely be displayed in bookstores and libraries stacked up with other books. Therefore you should place the title in the top third of the composition, and should design an interesting spine for the book as well. The text font should match the content and style of the story and illustrations. Feel free to have fun with it, but make sure that it reflects the tone of the story and doesn't send mixed messages to the reader.

Remember that the book cover will often be reduced to a thumbnail image for reviews and catalogues; the title should be large and legible.

Since the front cover illustration introduces the characters with a close-up, the back cover illustration can open up into a landscape and create text space.

A book's spine should include the author's name, the book title, the name of the series if there is one and the name of the publisher.

On this cover the title font matches the polar bear's fluffy fur and the falling snow.

In a picture book, the illustrator is responsible for the images on all 32 pages of the book, including the cover, retaining the same style of drawing and media throughout. Sometimes the image for the book jacket can be an image or a cropped image taken from the pages of the book, but mostly it is an image that has been designed specifically for the cover. In books for older children – especially in paperback form – there are often either no illustrations, or only black-and-white line illustrations. Jacket commissions may come with additional black and white illustrations required, so the whole book is produced by the same artist. However, it is quite common for the cover and the drawings inside a book to be illustrated by different artists, especially if the jacket is for an update of an existing book.

Foreign editions

Sometimes different covers will be produced for different markets – here, the Australian, Italian and French editions of the same book are shown.

Designing the type

Inside a book you will often be restricted to black type to make it easier for the publisher to sell to foreign markets. But on the cover (which is usually specific to a particular market) you will have the freedom to build coloured type into the design.

Illuminating historical facts
Illustrating facts that can't
be represented as photographs
is an important area for
illustrators (see page 108).

Chapter four

NON-FICTION

Writing and illustrating children's non-fiction is not simply about creating a shorter version of a book for adults. The whole concept is different and the presentation more direct. There is an art to writing and illustrating non-fiction for a young market, and there should be nothing prosaic about such work.

38 THE NON-FICTION MARKET

It is difficult for an unknown writer to break into publishing, and this is especially so for non-fiction, which is almost a closed shop. Nonetheless, there are still openings, especially for writers with fresh ideas for text-led, rather than design-led, books.

What sells?

Try to get hold of a publisher's catalogue to get a feel for the kinds of subjects that sell, year after year.

ORIGINATION OF IDEAS

Most non-fiction book ideas originate with the publisher. They may float an idea – with a makeshift cover and a couple of inside spreads – at the book fairs that are part of the annual publishing calendar. If buyers from the big bookshop chains and supermarkets are enthusiastic, the publisher will then hire a freelance writer to write the book to a specific brief.

WHO WRITES NON-FICTION?

Most children's non-fiction publishers consider it such a specialist market that they only employ writers with previous experience of this genre. Some will only employ people who have previously worked with them, regardless of their experience.

The reason publishers like to work with proven authors is fairly simple. Writing information books for children requires specialist knowledge. Unlike fiction, most information books are highly illustrated. Such books are often referred to as "integrated" – where words and pictures work together to provide information. A writer of such books need to understand how best to present information in this way. They often have to work closely with the book's designer, fitting text and captions around illustrations.

Former teachers are considered especially suitable for non-fiction writing. Publishers may also employ people who have some celebrity attached to the subject they are writing about – for example a well-known weatherman who appears on national television may be asked to write a book about weather.

Stiff competition

Over the last ten years the internet has become a serious rival to non-fiction books. Many children now make Google their first stop when researching homework, rather than the school library. The demand for information books has dropped. Because of this, bookshops have reduced display space. Profit margins have been squeezed and publishers have to contend with lower budgets for writers and illustrations. This is a vicious circle – it makes it more difficult for a book to appear exciting and "cool" compared to the audiovisual possibilities of the internet.

This is a disturbing trend, not least because the quality of information on the internet is unpredictable. Information books are carefully researched and written by a professional writer skilled in communicating with the reader. They will have been checked by an editor and an academic expert. A website, on the other hand, could have been written by an enthusiastic amateur or a blinkered obsessive. It takes a skill and maturity beyond the average school-age child to spot the sites that offer opinion or propaganda rather than even-handed information.

Bright sparks
Today's children are computer-literate from an early age. Your job is to spark their imagination and make sure they keep reading, too.

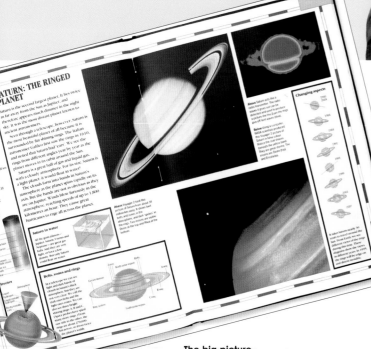

The big picture
Illustration and layout are essential to children's nonfiction. A good illustrator and designer will help you get your message across in an accessible way.

NEW APPROACHES

In the past, non-fiction has been seen as the worthy and dull end of the children's book market. More recently, publishers have had huge success with innovative illustration-led books, such as the *Eyewitness Guides* produced by Dorling Kindersley, and entertaining projects such as Scholastic's *Horrible Histories*.

The world of children's non-fiction is not completely closed to outsiders. If you can think of a new angle to a familiar subject, it is still worth approaching publishers. Find out about publishers who produce books in a similar field to your idea via your library, local bookshop, or a publishing directory, and contact them with a proposal.

STICK TO SCHOOL SUBJECTS

Information books that follow the school curriculum will be more likely to sell than those that do not. Your pet idea about aboriginal peoples in Southeast Asia is less likely to be considered, no matter how interesting, than one about the Civil War or the Industrial Revolution.

39 ILLUSTRATING NON-FICTION

Appealing illustrations are an essential ingredient of children's picture books, and this is also the case with non-fiction books. In making the book a desirable item to purchase, illustrations can have an impact far more immediate than the text. The standard of illustration across all children's publishing is invariably high and illustrators will usually be art-school graduates at the very least.

HOW ILLUSTRATORS WORK

Although artwork in a non-fiction book is central to its appeal, the illustrator will usually be given a much tighter brief than, for example, a picture book artist would. The content will be carefully planned out beforehand by the writer, editor and designer. The illustrator will then be sent a detailed brief with references, along with a spread worked up by the designer, showing exactly what the illustration needs to look like and how it will fit into the design of the book.

AGENTS

As an illustrator you will have to decide whether to approach publishers directly or employ an agent. Agents know their market, and they know how to match illustrators and publishing clients. They are often approached directly by publishers looking for a particular style of artwork, and they will be able to negotiate a fair rate for a particular piece of work. In return for these services they will charge around 15 per cent of your fee.

ILLUSTRATION STYLES

Non-fiction illustrators work in a variety of ways. Some produce colourful recreations of dramatic moments or everyday lives from history. Such artwork requires a serious knowledge of the period and many thoroughly researched references. Science and "how things work" books often feature a flatter, more diagrammatic style of artwork. Then there are alphabet and counting books for early learners, where the illustrator's work will be the major selling point of the book. On the edge of the non-fiction illustration genre are puzzle books, such as the hugely successful *Where's Wally* series by Martin Handford (1987).

Age and subject matter
Non-fiction illustrations can vary in complexity, depending on the age of the reader and the subject matter, as shown in these book spreads.

bits and Bear care

Cartoon care
This non-fiction book illustration relies on simple drawings of a cartoon bear to demonstrate how a young reader should care for their body.

You may prefer not to go through an agent and to approach publishers directly. This can be an uphill struggle for anyone straight out of art college. You will need to identify the kind of publisher who produces books using your style of artwork. Then you need to contact the art director or creative director there and send photocopied or printed samples of your work. You can find out the name of the person you need to approach by consulting publishing directories such as the *Children's Writers' & Artists' Yearbook* (A&C Black Publishers). This is published annually, so be sure to use the latest edition.

GLOBAL MARKETS

Most information books need to have international sales potential. European publishers especially will not make a profit based solely on sales in their own country, so artwork needs to have a universal appeal. Cars, for example, should be shown with reflections on the windshield that do not allow the reader to see the left-hand or right-hand position of the driver. Whichever side you draw, one will look wrong in some of the countries where the book will be sold.

Nudity is also a problem – even a rear view that shows only the buttocks. In many European countries a cartoon depiction of a child getting out of a bath or an artwork recreation of semi-naked Neolithic people would go unquestioned, but in the United States such illustrations are unacceptable.

Extra elements
Besides an increase in sophistication and detail, illustrations for older readers often include elements such as diagrams and maps.

40 WRITING FOR DIFFERENT AGES

Information books follow all the rules for age-level that apply to picture books and fiction. You need to constantly be aware of your reader's level of understanding and vocabulary. Sentences must be short – aim for under 20 words – without complex clauses, and with an unambiguous clarity.

Ageless appeal
The ancient Egyptians provide an example of a non-fiction subject that continues to fascinate readers of all ages.

ASSUMED KNOWLEDGE

The easiest trap to fall into when writing non-fiction is to assume a knowledge that the reader hasn't got. This is why some non-fiction publishers prefer to use general writers rather than specialists. A lifelong sailor writing about sailing ships, for example, might assume that everyone knows what "port" and "starboard" mean, or what the "mizzenmast" or "yardarms" are. After all, these are terms they may use every day. But most children will be baffled by these unfamiliar words and quickly lose interest in the book.

Likewise, a historian who spends his professional life writing or lecturing about the Second World War will assume everyone knows who Stalin, Churchill or Roosevelt are. This is not the case, even for teenage children. Phrases such as "Britain's wartime prime minister Winston Churchill..." or "American president Franklin D. Roosevelt..." will succinctly remind your reader who these people are.

Glossaries

Many non-fiction books have a glossary at the back. This is useful for providing handy definitions of complicated and unfamiliar words, but don't assume a reader will use it. Most children will quickly grow tired of having to look up words at the back of the book – that's assuming they know there's a glossary there in the first place. You need to explain unfamiliar words clearly when you first use them.

PITCH TO AGE

As with other children's genres, non-fiction books fall into categories determined by age range. For pre-school children there are broad introductions to the world of history or science, for example. Books for elementary school children will have more specific subjects such as baby animals, how flowers grow or what happens to our refuse. Information books for older children may consider the Holocaust or systems of government such as democracy or dictatorship. Such books change in complexity and sophistication as the target age grows older.

WHO'S WHO

Younger children have no clear understanding of the chronological framework of history. They often get historical figures mixed up, asking such questions as "Is Hitler the one who had his wives' heads chopped off?"

SCHOOL SUBJECTS

Government and education authorities post information on the internet about which subjects are covered by the school curriculum, and the age children are when they study them. For example, primary school children often study the ancient cultures of Egypt, Greece and Rome, so books about these eras are often pitched at the younger end of the non-fiction market. The Second World War may be studied in detail by secondary school children, so information books about that are pitched at early teens and older.

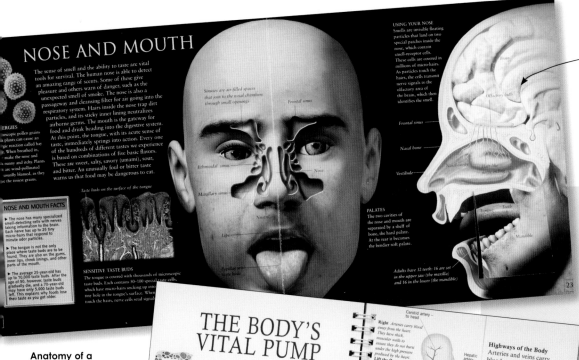

When you generate your text you will need to give suggestions for how it could be illustrated. Every illustration will need a hard-working caption and details of the image may also be annotated with numbered captions or leader lines.

CONTRAST AND COMPARE!

Below are two strikingly different approaches to the subject of sneezing. Both contain the same number of key facts; only one of them is entertaining, and that's the one pitched at children.

Adult non-fiction

A sternutation, commonly known as "a sneeze", is a paroxysmal expulsion of air from the lungs. It is caused by foreign matter irritating the nasal mucus. In the case of the "photic sneeze reflex", sneezing may also be caused by exposure to bright light.

Child's non-fiction

What travels at 100 miles (150 km) per hour? Your snot! Every time you sneeze, mucus is pushed out of your nose at this amazing speed. How come you've never noticed? Because every time you sneeze, you shut your eyes. Go on – try to sneeze and keep your eyes open. It's impossible! Here's another challenge; try saying the word "sternutation". It's a biggie, isn't it? That's the official word for a sneeze. But you're probably still asking: what makes me sneeze? It can be anything from dust to pollen, a cold to sudden light. Make sure you duck next time your friend feels a sneeze coming on. You don't want an unwelcome shower!

Anatomy of a non-fiction book

Non-fiction books (for all ages) follow some fairly standard conventions that you won't find in fiction. You will need to consider these in your writing.

Most non-fiction books are divided into sections, chapters or double-page spreads. Each will need an introductory paragraph or standfirst.

The main thrust of the article is contained in the body text, which is further subdivided under headings. Remember, though, that the reader may never get beyond the captions!

Illustrations are usually commissioned after the text has been written, based on your image suggestions. The editor may ask you to provide reference for the artist.

41
NARRATIVE NON-FICTION

Narrative or "creative" non-fiction is a way of relating real-life events with the immediacy, emotional involvement and power of a novel. It is what journalist and novelist Edward Humes brilliantly describes as "the art of being there". As this is very much a text-led (rather than design- or illustration-led) genre, it provides a promising avenue for new writers trying to break into children's non-fiction to explore.

TRICKS FROM TELEVISION

Television documentary makers have long used this technique to create "faction" or "docudrama" programs about real events – with actors used to depict scenes based closely on real life. In narrative non-fiction, a writer will employ many of the techniques of fiction – lively dialogue, evocative descriptions, glimpses into the secret thoughts and motives of his characters – to weave a story the reader will be drawn into.

WATCH WHAT YOU SAY

In narrative non-fiction, in any story set in even the recent past, you need to think dialogue through carefully. Although many children will not understand archaic speech forms and vocabulary, you need to aim to create speech which at least sounds authentic and of its time. In all but the most recent stories you would naturally avoid obvious slang words such as "dude" or "cool". But take care also not to use modern idioms such as "Check out..." (as in "check out those English archers on our flank, your Majesty!").

NON-FICTION SUBJECTS WORTH EXPLORING

- History with a twist – entertaining real-life characters and pivotal moments in history would all be good jumping-off points.

- Practical science – children love getting their hands dirty with (safe) experiments to try at home.

- Green issues – this subject is very hot right now and and unlikely to cool off in the near future.

- How to have fun – how can you teach readers without it feeling like a lesson? Turn your book into a big game.

- Anything scatological – children love it!

OVER-PUBLISHED NON-FICTION AREAS

- Curriculum subjects are often heavily published! They can guarantee sales, but can you find a new way to approach familiar subjects?

Writing non-fiction
Your non-fiction writing will undoubtedly be influenced by what children are studying in the classroom. Take the time to research what teachers, librarians and parents are looking for – and then have fun.

What makes for great non-fiction?
Creating a truly great non-fiction book demands an innovative approach – but beyond that, the genre is difficult to categorize, as this list of great examples demonstrates.

USING CHARACTERS

Narrative non-fiction offers an attractive freedom to a writer. A story about the Battle of Iwo Jima or the Somme, for example, may start with fresh recruits waiting for a train that will take them away from home. What are they thinking? Are they fearful or excited? Are some keen to escape their dull small-town lives, or are they already missing the wives or sweethearts they have left behind? If the reader cares about the characters in the story they will be engrossed in the struggles and challenges they have to face.

RESEARCH

Writing narrative non-fiction properly requires a level of empathy and research similar to that demanded by historical fiction – in fact, the genres are remarkably similar. The main difference is that the narrative non-fiction writer must stick rigorously to portraying real people and events, while the fiction writer can be more creative with both their characters and the known facts.

Constantly ask yourself questions such as, "How would this feel?" or "What would they be thinking?" As well as reading around the subject, trips to relevant museums and sites of historical importance will be invaluable in helping you gain an understanding of what it was like to be the people you are writing about. Living museums, such as the Plimoth Plantation in Plymouth, Massachusetts will provide any writer with many chapters' worth of material.

BROAD SPECTRUM

Narrative non-fiction is particularly well suited to subjects popular with boys: adventure stories of survival, exploration and heroism; great events in history; and war stories. But recently the genre has been successfully applied to tales of scientific discovery and even advances in mathematics!

FIVE GREAT NON-FICTION BOOKS:

1. *Horrible Histories by Terry Deary*
(first book published 1993)
This massively popular paperback series of children's nonfiction uses humour, gore and cartoon illustration to bring subjects to life.

2. *The Way Things Work by David Macaulay*
(1988)
Highly illustrated cross-sections of everything from a car transmission to a body-scanner.

3. *The Grossology series by Sylvia Branzei*
(1995)
Covering subjects such as animals, the human body, and food these books use the "yuk-factor" to appeal to children.

4. *The Wizardology series by Dugald Steer*
(2005)
Full of special features and puzzles, these innovative books get young minds working hard.

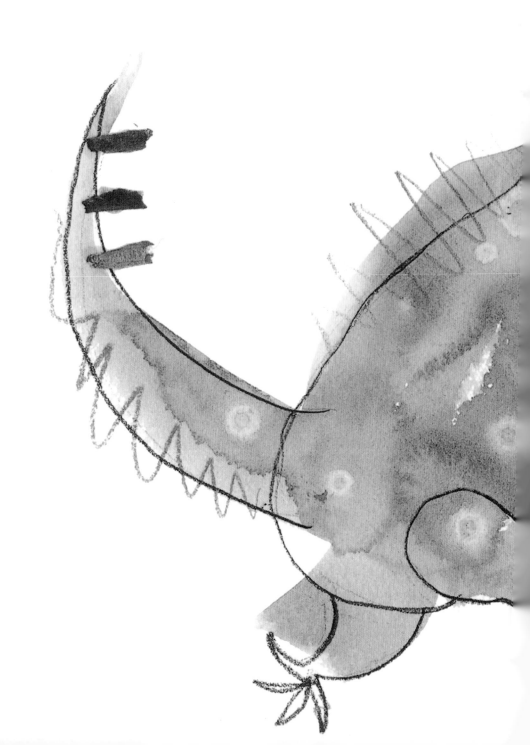

USING WATERCOLOUR WASHES
Watercolour is great for creating gentle colour gradations (see page 124).

Chapter five

MEDIA AND TECHNIQUES

A step-by-step refresher course demonstrating some of the most important media characteristics and how to exploit them to create wonderful and compelling artwork.

GALLERY OF TECHNIQUES

The gallery of images on these pages provides an overview of the diverse illustration techniques explained in more detail in this chapter.

DRY COLOUR

Pastels
Here, coloured pencils were used to create a sensitive line drawing, and then soft chalk pastels were blended over the top to create a soft, dusty texture.

TRANSLUCENT

Watercolour
Watercolour is a popular medium. The white of the paper can be used to exploit the transparency of the watercolour over the delicate pencil drawing.

Inks
Simple pen and ink drawings are rendered with vibrant washes of watercolour inks.

BLACK AND WHITE

Crosshatching
Here, the artist used a technical drawing pen and built up tone mechanically with crosshatched lines.

Brush pen
Black watercolour was used to create strong, simple shapes and patterns, washed over in places.

Flat black
A drawing was scanned into the computer and the solid areas were filled in using Photoshop.

MIXED MEDIA

Many media
This artwork is a combination of pen and ink drawing with watercolour, coloured pencils, pastels and gouache layers, creating a textured effect.

DIGITAL

Digitally manipulated
These graphic line drawings were scanned, flat colour was dropped into areas using Photoshop, and then printed on coloured paper.

Brushes
A good starter kit includes: three round brushes (left) for detail
and washes; a flat brush (center) for lines; two rigger brushes
(right) for fine details; and a pointed mop brush (far right).

43 TRANSLUCENT

Using translucent watercolour media is possibly
the most popular illustration technique for children's
illustration. It offers fresh, bright colour and can be simple or
sophisticated in its application. Paint can be used directly
as a wash, but mostly it is combined with a pencil or ink line.

WATERCOLOUR MEDIA

Watercolour pans provide more
concentrated colour than
tubes. This is because the paint
in tubes contains more binding
ingredient to keep the pigment
soft. Despite the dulling effect,
tubes are convenient to use for
mixing large amounts of paint
for washes.

Watercolour inks are synthetic
dyes and have real strength
and vibrancy. Even when
diluted quite considerably, they
still stain the paper and cannot
be lifted off with clean water
as watercolour paint can.

Both paints and inks make
use of the white of the
paper to add highlights, and
successful application relies on
confidence and spontaneity.
The translucent effect makes
these media more unforgiving
than many others. Learning
to control flat and gradient
washes, and practising mark-
making using items such as
rock salt and clingfilm, will

help you to appreciate the
versatility and control that
is possible. There is a great
number of books with useful
guidelines for using these
media, but look at more than
one. Many refer to particular
styles of working – remember
that you are in the process of
discovering your own!

Liquid acrylic inks

Liquid acrylic inks and liquid watercolours
Liquid acrylic inks and liquid watercolours are available in a wide range of
colours. They can be expensive when used at full strength but provide vibrant,
waterproof coverage. The acrylic inks are also lightfast when dry.

TOOLS FOR TRANSLUCENT MEDIA

Brushes: Nylon brushes are fine,
but expensive sable brushes are
perfect for watercolour. Use a
variety of sizes to carry the
watercolour, according to the task
– large, flat brushes for
backgrounds, and round brushes
for "filling in". Take care of your
brushes to retain their shape and

Liquid watercolour

prolong their life. Keep water clean
when mixing and rinsing (use two
pots) and don't leave brushes
standing in water, as it will damage
their tips. Use white tissue to check
that a brush is cleaned of pigment
before mixing another colour.

Paper: Stretch paper if it is
lightweight, or if you are going
to apply a considerable amount
of watercolour, to avoid buckling
and the formation of puddles.
Using good quality, professional
watercolour paper will make a
difference to the application of
washes and colour. Experiment
with the range of "hot press",
"not" and "rough" papers to
see what suits you best.

Masking: Masking fluid helps
to protect small areas of paper
while you apply washes, and
masking film is excellent for larger
areas. Wax-resist leaves a soft,
broken mark to retain lighter areas,
but this is of course permanent.
Masking tape works, but does
have a tendency to rip the paper.

*Traditional watercolour paints
in tubes and pans*

PAPER TEXTURES

Watercolour paper is made in different weights and textures. Because watercolour techniques rely so much on the texture of paper, it is important to choose the best one for your own style.

Watercolour board: As its name suggests, watercolour board is watercolour paper attached to board. It is very useful when you don't want – or have no time – to stretch paper.

Hot-pressed: This paper has a smooth surface, making it ideal for highly detailed work.

Not: This term is short for "not hot-pressed". The paper has a gently textured surface.

Rough: This paper is suitable for broad, expressive work and wet washes.

Handmade papers: These are produced in all kinds of textures, making them ideal for individual, experimental techniques.

STRETCHING PAPER

Paper has a truly infuriating tendency to buckle when water is applied to the surface, particularly the lighter weights. When you are trying to produce an illustration, this does not enhance its professional appearance. By stretching your paper, you should avoid a wrinkled finished piece.

Tools and materials
- Watercolour paper of your choice
- Wooden drawing board at least 5 cm (2 in) bigger around than the paper
- Large, flat-bottomed washing up bowl (or you can use the bathtub)
- Natural or synthetic sponge
- Gummed paper strips cut to the right lengths a little longer than the edges of the paper
- Scissors

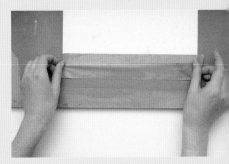

1 Watercolour paper is one-sided, and it is very important that you remember which the right side is – initially the watermark will show you (it will read correctly from the right side). Immerse the paper completely in clean, cold water for a few minutes.

2 Lay the paper, right side up, onto a clean wooden drawing board. Start at one edge and press it down. With a clean sponge, stroke the paper gently in one direction to remove any air bubbles that have formed between the paper and the board.

3 Remove any excess water with a squeezed-out dry sponge and then seal the edges of the paper with gummed tape. Tear a length a little longer than one side of the paper and stroke it with the wet sponge to activate the glue. Take care not to under-or over-soak it.

4 Lay the gummed paper strip so that it covers the edge of the watercolour paper. Repeat for all four sides. You can add small corner pieces to prevent the strip from lifting at the corners. Leave the paper to dry in a warm place – it must be totally dry before it is used. Stretching the paper yourself is a lengthy process; pre-stretched paper provides a much quicker, though more expensive, option.

MIXING PAINT

When you use watercolours or gouache, the most important consideration is how much pigment to mix with the water. Obviously, this effects how translucent the colour will be – the more water, the more transparent the colour. Gouache is much thicker, but if mixed with increasing quantities of water it can take on the qualities of watercolour. Meanwhile, some of the chalkier watercolour pigments, such as lemon yellow or cadmium red, can take on an opaque appearance if mixed only sparingly with water. Be careful not to use too much paint though, which will cause your work to look heavy and dull.

Paint consistency

Experiment by mixing in the palette and then painting with varying degrees of water. **Top left and right:** a very thin wash mixed with a lot of water and a little pigment (either watercolour or gouache) – this would probably be too weak for a whole painting, although would work well if used in conjunction with a holding line. **Centre left and right:** the classic watercolour strength – there is enough pigment in the mix for the colour to become luminescent when the white of the paper shows through. **Bottom left and right:** a thicker mix suitable for dry brushwork or for when you want an opaque effect.

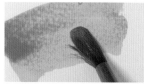
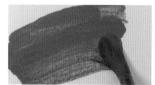

MIXING COLOURS

Colour mixing can be done either in the palette or on the paper. There are two considerations: first, how much to mix – this will come with experience. If you are painting a large area, mix more than you think you will need if colour consistency is important, as you will never manage to match the colour if you run out. Second, the tone of the colours will affect how much of each to use.

Blending on paper

These colours (sap green and cadmium yellow) were mixed by blending them together on the paper.

Glazing

In a traditional method known as "glazing", layers of transparent colour are washed, one over another. This example (right) shows cadmium yellow over cerulean blue. The colours are optically mixed to give a fresh green.

Mixing in a palette

You can mix paint in a palette (right) and add water, which will allow you to fine-tune the colours. Start with the paler tone (lemon yellow) and add tiny quantities of the darker tone (cobalt blue). Keep adding blue until you have achieved the desired shade of green. If you started with the darker tone and mixed in the paler one it would take far more paint to achieve the same colour.

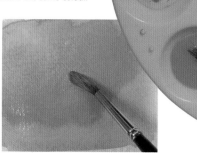

WASHES

The fundametal technique of watercolour is to lay a single-colour, flat wash that is useful for backgrounds, skies or as a basis for a wash containing two or more colours. A wash can be applied in a controlled way as shown in the first example, or in a looser way as in the second example, where a second colour is dropped on wet, and allowed to bleed into the first.

Flat wash Load a large wash brush with paint and make a horizontal stroke. Paint will collect at the bottom. Make more strokes, each overlapping the last, until you have covered the desired area.

Gradated wash Similar to the flat wash, thin the paint with more water after every stroke to make a fading wash to white.

Variegated wash Start by making a flat wash. Where you would like to change colour, start applying the second colour with a clean brush. The two colours will blend with unpredictable results.

WET-ON-DRY

For detailed work, a technique called wet-on-dry is used. The initial wash is left to dry and then the detail is painted on top. Don't press too hard or scrub at the paper to avoid moving the pigment from the first wash; the colours may become muddy, and you will lose any detail you are trying to capture. Using watercolour pigments or inks for the first wash helps as they are less likely to move later.

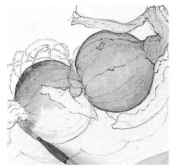

1 Draw your image faintly with a pencil, then fill the brush and wet the whole area inside the outline. You need to be accurate to achieve a clean edge.

2 Add colour in layers, starting with the palest, and allowing the pigments to mix on the paper. Keep in mind where you want highlights, and work dark areas around them.

TRY THIS

Follow the techniques listed here as you draw and paint simple household objects as reference.

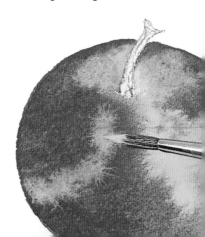

Wet on dry
Very fine wet-on-dry brushwork achieved this level of detail.

WET-IN-WET

As you will be working with lots of water, there is a risk of the paper buckling. To prevent this, either use a heavy paper – at least 160 lb (340 gsm) – or stretch the paper (see page 119). Rough textures give the best results. Use large brushes to deliver the maximum amount of pigment and water.

1 Draw the outline of the image faintly with a pencil, then fill the brush and wet the whole area inside the outline. You need to be accurate to achieve a clean edge.

2 Add the colour in layers, starting with the palest washes and allowing the pigment to mix on the paper. Keep in mind where you wish the highlights to be, and work the dark areas around them.

3 Try to keep the whole area as wet as possible by using very watery washes. This helps the layers of colour to mix softly without leaving hard edges.

MASKING

Masking, or preserving, the white of the paper as a highlight is an important technique for illustrators working in transparent media. This is because the white of the paper is always brighter and whiter than white paint would be, so your highlights will sparkle. It also allows you to freely apply washes over the illustration while the masked highlights are protected.

Masks are especially useful if you want to create flat background washes or variegated washes behind characters or objects in the foreground. You will have discovered that if you try to paint around an object, the paint will dry before you finish, which makes it impossible to achieve a flat background. Use film or masking fluid to block out areas: film for larger areas and masking fluid for details or highlights.

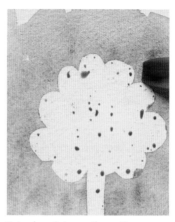

1 To mask an area with film, place transparent sticky-backed film over the drawn image, and use a sharp craft knife or scalpel to cut it out.

2 Apply paint over the entire area with a large brush, working from the centre to the left and right. Don't scrub around the film edges.

3 Leave the wash to dry completely before you remove the film. You may need to use a scalpel to help you lift the edge of the film.

1 To mask an area with masking fluid, sketch in the design lightly with a pencil first. Apply the masking fluid with an old brush – it can be difficult to remove from the bristles afterwards.

2 Make sure the fluid is completely dry before applying any paint. This technique can be used with any waterbased pigment and, as in this example, is extremely successful with watercolour.

3 Once the paint has dried, remove the fluid with a clean finger or an eraser. Any pencil marks under the fluid will be removed, leaving a clean, white area. Masking fluid can also be used over a dry wash to protect it from the next layer.

EDGE MASKING

Masking tape can be used to achieve crisp edges around your illustration. Take care not to damage the paper when you peel off the tape.

1 Before applying masking tape, measure the dimensions of your illustration and pencil in the area lightly (use a triangle to ensure right angles). Carefully lay down the masking tape, pressing down the inside edge only, and taking particular care at the corners. Make sure there are no air pockets on or near the edge to be painted, or the paint will seep under. Add the wash as usual.

2 Allow paint to dry completely. Carefully peel back the masking tape to reveal the edge. Do not leave the tape in place for too long as it will eventually stain the paper.

SCRATCHING OUT

You may have to work to tight deadlines, so techniques that can speed up your work can be very handy. Keeping small areas for white highlights can be difficult when you are working at speed. "Scratching out" with a blade after the paint has dried is a quick and effective method of reclaiming highlights. (Alternative methods include using opaque white paint such as gouache, or masking fluid.)

This technique is particularly suitable for fine-line highlights. It should only be used on heavier papers – 300 gsm (140 lb) or over – as it is possible to make holes in thin ones.

SPONGING

Sponging is a very expressive method that is quick to master and is ideal for experimentation. It can be used on its own to build a complete image, or combined with other watercolour techniques.

1 A small natural sponge is the ideal tool for this technique. It is used quite dry on a rough-surfaced paper to produce a highly textured effect.

Before
After

For straight lines, a little metal ruler is useful to guide your hand. Drag the scalpel lightly at first, repeating the process until you achieve the amount of highlight required.

2 The great value of the sponging technique is that it creates a complete image that is both evocative and decorative in a very short time – always a bonus for a busy illustrator.

READ THESE

An Introduction to Watercolour
by Ray Smith (1993)

The Encyclopedia of Watercolour Techniques: A Step-by-Step Visual Directory
by Hazel Harrison (2004)

LINE AND WASH

The line and wash technique allows the creation of a complete image extremely quickly, and has been the preferred medium for many famous illustrators. It combines two traditional techniques: pen and ink and watercolour. Flat wash tints are applied over an ink line drawing.

BASIC EQUIPMENT

It is very important to choose the correct paper for the line and wash technique. It must be strong enough to resist cockling when washed, yet smooth enough to take a pen line. Smooth "not" watercolour papers fulfill these criteria; experiment with different types until you find the one that suits your style.

Traditional watercolour pigments and brushes are used to create the washes, while the drawing is done with a dip pen. There is a wide range of nibs available that produce different widths and qualities of lines. You

will need to use waterproof ink – it has a tendency to dry quickly, so you will need to clean the nib regularly to keep it from clogging.

GETTING STARTED

There are three approaches to this technique; the most traditional is to start with the ink drawing. When the ink is completely dry, thin colour washes are applied. Greater intensity of colour can be built up using successive layers, or by working wet-in-wet (see page 123). The second method is to apply the washes first and, once dry, add the ink drawing afterwards. The third involves working up the two elements together, adding more line and colour where necessary.

The key to success with this technique is the integration of the colour with the line. Experiment with applying the washes, keeping them wet and loose, and allowing them to break out of the ink lines.

Inks and pens
For linework, use black or brown waterproof ink and a dip pen (above). Apply washes of colour using inks or watercolour (below).

Putty erasers
For erasing the pencil line, putty erasers are superior to traditional erasers as they do not leave rubbings.

TRADITIONAL METHOD

Remember to use waterproof ink, as washes are added over the linework. Use pre-stretched watercolour paper with a smooth surface for this technique.

1 Outline the original drawing lightly in pencil as a guide for the dip-pen line work that will be added over the top. (Once dry, any visible pencil lines can be removed with a putty eraser.)

ALTERNATIVE METHOD

An alternative line and wash method involves laying down the washes first, with the linework added with a dip pen when they have dried. You will discover in time which technique suits you best.

1 Outline the design with a faint pencil line. Apply masking fluid with an old brush to the areas that are to be reserved as white paper. Allow the masking fluid to dry (this may take a few minutes).

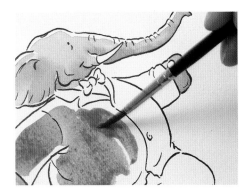

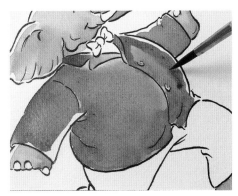

2 Using the pencil lines as a guide, apply the watercolour washes with a sable brush. Two tones of each colour are mixed, and the palest is applied first.

3 Before the first wash is completely dry, add the second, darker wash. This darker wash (applied here to the outside edge of the coat), will help to emphasize the elephant's rotund figure. Because the first wash is quite dry, the two tones blend slightly, merging along the soft edge.

4 This technique of two-tone washes is used to complete the whole illustration. It is important not to overwork the colour, as you may lose the fresh, spontaneous feel characteristic of this technique.

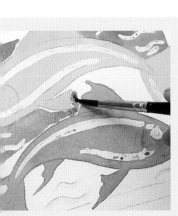

2 Wash over the fish and the background water with a sable brush. At this stage add only the basic wash for each area. Shadow washes can be added later.

3 Once the washes have dried, the masking fluid can be removed with a putty eraser, leaving the highlights on the backs of the fish and in the water. The lines can then be added with dip pen and waterproof ink.

4 A more three-dimensional quality can be added to selected areas of the design once the linework has dried by adding a second, darker wash.

DRY COLOUR

Pastels are perfect for producing bold, rich and expressive illustrations. This is also true of watercolour-based pencils, except that pastels, unlike pencil crayons, are not really suitable for small-scale work.

CRAYONS AND PASTELS

Traditional coloured pencils or crayons create a softer quality of image than pastels. They are perfect for sketching and visualizing.

Pastels come in two types – oil and chalk (or soft) pastels – and in a range of qualities from soft (with more pigment) to hard (with more binder). Most pastel work is done on tinted rather than white paper as the process of application is through blending; working light to dark or dark to light. White and light colours can give powerful highlights, and light is often an important element in pastel work.

Oil pastels are more difficult to work with but the density of the colour gives a much richer effect. Scale can be a problem for scanning and, as the artwork is necessarily large, details may be lost on reduction. Faces can be difficult to keep attractive and manageable on a small scale. Turpentine can create a wonderful painterly effect, with the opportunity to scratch into the oily surface when applied thickly or to leave it with an impasto effect.

COLOUR MIXES AND "WASHES"

With dry media, always lay the light colours first and then build up the image with the colours getting progressively darker. You will need a good range of colours for any dry media, as they cannot be mixed like paint; though you can overlap colours through a blending or crosshatching technique (see page 127). Only certain media will create a wash effect; use water to bleed watercolour pencils, or turpentine applied with a brush over oil pastels.

PAPER SURFACE

The results that are achievable with dry media vary dramatically depending on the type of paper used. With smooth papers, the pigment within the media covers the whole surface evenly; with rougher papers, it only adheres to the raised areas and therefore less pigment is laid down on the surface.

1 Coloured pencils

Although coloured pencils are easy to use, they have the potential to produce very rich and vibrant images. Some artists apply a watercolour wash first, to tint the paper. For detailed work, hot pressed paper is best. For looser work, a slightly rougher paper can be used.

2 Oil pastels

Colours can be built up by layering one on top of another, using a series of marks – this is called "feathering". Blend oil pastels with your fingers or a torchon. Scratch into the surface, using a sharp tool or the end of a brush, to expose layers beneath and create a linear drawing. Blend with a solvent such as turpentine to give a smoother, more painterly effect, using a rag or a brush. Oil pastels will work with most paper surfaces, but specialist pastel papers are available.

3 Chalk pastels

Colours can be built up by applying the lightest tone first on a slightly tinted paper, then blending it with your finger or a torchon to create a smooth area of colour. Darker colours are placed over the top, blended again to create a smooth effect. As you apply more layers of colour you will see how each layer enriches the next and how you can create a variety of rich tones. You can also draw lines with pastels.

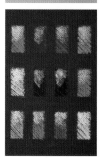

Coloured papers

Even though pastels provide a relatively opaque finish, the colour of the background paper still has a startling effect on perception of their colours.

DRY MEDIA STROKES

The strokes or marks made by the two types of pastel and coloured pencils are fairly similar. An entire picture may be built up using a network of lines, known as "hatching". Applied evenly and repeatedly these lines can create various gradated tones of colour, or may be left as angled strokes. These can then be overlaid with another layer of lines at a different angle – called "crosshatching". At any point a second or third colour may be introduced and blended, or hatched, over the base layer. These examples are some of the possible options.

Hatching and crosshatching: Long, diagonal hatched lines can be used to create form, or as a base layer (above). Two-colour crosshatching (above right) – shorter yellow lines over the longer lines of the first layer create a more varied surface texture. Two-colour short-line crosshatching (above far right), the red and blue forming small units. Crosshatching using the side of a pastel stick (right) at shallow angles. The variables of colour and length and angle of strokes give infinite variety.

Right: Subtle transitional blending of two colours can be achieved by careful (and time-consuming) building up of the pigment on the surface. A light, even pressure is required. Hold the pencil or pastel at an angle so that the point or edge does not create a visible line. Lay down the faintest layers first so that the pigment is just dusting the surface.

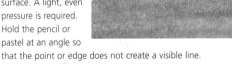

Top: Using the side of a pastel creates swaths of flat colour.

Above: Using a mid-toned grey paper adds an extra layer of colour.

Above: Feathering the marks gives interesting textures. Here, a red pastel is feathered over a magenta background.

Above right: Lightly blending softens the surface.

Right: Brushing liquid medium onto oil pastel is another way to vary the surface texture.

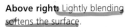

Left: A single colour may be blended with a finger.

Right: Here, two colours are blended with a finger.

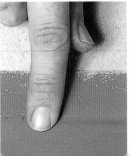

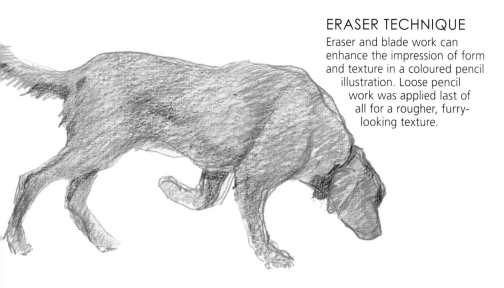

ERASER TECHNIQUE

Eraser and blade work can enhance the impression of form and texture in a coloured pencil illustration. Loose pencil work was applied last of all for a rougher, furry-looking texture.

1 The outline of the dog is drawn on smooth paper. The shape of the animal is then roughly modeled.

2 To brighten the highlight areas on the flanks and shoulders, the colour is scraped back with the blade of a scalpel.

3 A plastic eraser is used for cleaning up the drawing and burnishing the highlight areas.

BLENDING CHALK PASTEL

Because of the lovely, soft nature of chalk pastel, it is an ideal medium for decorative, impressionistic illustrations created with blending techniques. A wide variety of papers are suitable as backgrounds, including highly textured and coloured ones.

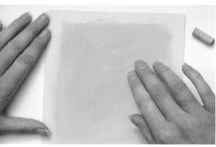

1 Over a creamy-yellow textured pastel paper, apply the background yellow with a short length of chalk used horizontally. Blend the pastel surface gently with the pads of your fingers and blow off any excess chalk.

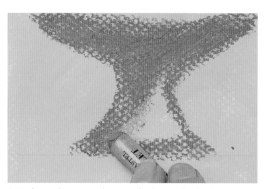

2 Darker colours are then applied over the background. Note how the texture of the paper breaks up the pastel strokes to create optical blending. This time your blending finger both softens the pastel strokes and blends the colours together. Pastel work is messy, so blend with a paper stump or torchon if you prefer.

3 When the work is completed it is vital to use a fixative to prevent unwanted smudging. This bonds the pastel to the paper.

OIL PASTEL: BLEND AND REVEAL

As an illustration technique, reveal can be extremely effective. You may find that warming the pastels gently before use will help soften them. This will help you to build up the amount of pigment on the paper necessary for this technique.

1, 2 Build up a thick layer of blended colours. Next, cover this with a darker layer of colour.

3 With a blunt point such as the end of a paintbrush, the design can then be scratched into the surface, revealing the under-layer. The line thickness depends on the tool you use.

OIL PASTEL: USING SOLVENTS

Although oil pastels have a thick, waxy texture, they can be worked into with a solvent to produce thin, transparent washes. Oil pastels are soluble in turpentine or mineral spirits. A variety of techniques can be used. The paper can be soaked first in turpentine or oil and then drawn on or, as in this example, the pastel drawing can be worked into with the solvent.

1 Starting with pale colours, build up an under-layer of mixed tones. Rough paper is particularly suitable as it helps you to apply a thicker layer of pastel and catches the under-layer in its depressions so that it, and not the paper, is revealed.

2 The turpentine or mineral spirits is applied to a clean tissue or piece of paper towel, which is then used to blend and spread the colour over the image with small, circular strokes.

3 Allow the solvent to dry, and then pass more pastel over the top; if the paper remains wet, the overlaid pastel will bleed, making the line fuzzy. You can deliberately exploit this property to produce interesting results.

4 Further blending can be done with a finger and the solvent-soaked paper towel, gradually building up the image. For small, detailed areas, a cotton swab soaked in turpentine may be used.

BLACK AND WHITE

Black-and-white illustrations are usually associated with longer storybooks and novels, in which the illustrations accompany and break up a large body of text. This discipline is still very important in children's illustration but it is often neglected in portfolios. It can be a good way of entering the field and getting your work published.

Scraperboard is a method in which a black surface is scratched away to reveal white beneath.

READ THESE

There are many books that will give you technical advice on the variety of media for drawing. Try the following:

The Manual of Illustration Techniques by Catherine Slade (2003)

The Pen and Ink Book by J. A. Smith (1999)

TOOLS FOR BLACK AND WHITE

There is a vast range of tools that can be used to create black-and-white images, including: fibre-tip pens, fountain pens, rollerball pens, technical pens and ballpoint pens. Most of these tools create a line that is even in weight and thickness.

Graphite pencils or sticks, conté pencils, oil pastels, chalk pastels and charcoal can all be used to create more subtle tonal qualities and monochromatic images, including half-tone.

Scraperboard is a white, chalky material that has been coated with black ink. Various tools are used to scratch into the black surface, exposing the white beneath. Tools can vary from special scraperboard nibs to anything sharp such as a scalpel, a nail, or a pin.

Consistent tone: The side of the point creates consistent tone.

Varied tone: Varied pressure on the point results in altered tone.

Hatching: Hatching and crosshatching build controlled tone.

Blending: Soft graphite can be blended with a finger.

Texture: A single soft pencil is capable of a wide visual vocabulary.

Erasing: An eraser can be used to produce tonal or textural effects.

Coverage: A thick stick of charcoal on its side can cover an area quickly.

Soft marks: Putty erasers can create soft marks for a ghostlike effect.

Hard marks: A hard, vinyl eraser makes sharper, more precise marks.

SILHOUETTE DRAWING

Silhouette drawing has always been a popular style for children's books. Perhaps the most famous practitioner of this style was Arthur Rackham, who used it to create detailed, magical illustrations for books like *Rip Van Winkle*. For a crisp edge to your silhouette, start by creating an outline drawing.

1 Use a light pencil to outline the image. Then retrace it with the dip pen. When the ink runs out, re-dip the pen. If there is too much ink in the pen, it will blot, so do a small test on a separate sheet to prevent accidents.

2 When the ink is completely dry, any pencil marks showing can be erased using a putty eraser.

3 Use a small brush and the same ink to fill in the outline to create a silhouette. Paint around the eyes of the octopus to give him character. You can speed up the drying time of the ink with a hairdryer. Be careful that it is not too hot or held too close or it may buckle the paper.

4 The finished silhouette.

CONTOUR DRAWING

With contour drawing, a subject is described by varying the outline. By making the outline thinner or thicker, rigid or soft, continuous or broken, the difference between materials can be expressed. This is achieved by using the flexibility of the nib of a dip pen. A light amount of pressure with lines at a distance apart creates lighter shading. More pressure and closer lines make darker tones.

1 The overall design is drawn lightly in pencil. It is then retraced using a dip pen; vary the line, and therefore describe the subject, by applying more or less pressure. Look closely at how the folds in the sleeves are created with a variation in thickness of the line.

2 The whole figure is outlined in this method, allowing the line to tail off gradually by releasing the pressure on the nib. The softness and movement of the fabric can be expressed with a broken line.

3 When the ink is dry, using a thinner nib and working from the top, add in shading by crosshatching. With contour drawing the lines must follow the form of the object it is describing. As the umbrella is reserved, the lines are drawn to follow its contours.

4 Contour drawing is a very similar method to crosshatching, but as can be seen from the example, the quality of this technique is freer and more expressive.

MIXED MEDIA AND COLLAGE

Combining different media and materials together has become very popular. It naturally encourages an imaginative and innovative approach to image-making.

TYPES OF MIXED MEDIA

"Mixed media" is traditionally a combination of painting and drawing techniques using a variety of media. This has developed into a more complex combination, with the addition of printmaking, photography, bas-relief and collage.

COLLAGE POSSIBILITIES

Collage is the gluing together of a variety of materials – though mainly paper – onto a surface to create an image. Perhaps the most well-known use of collage in children's book illustration is by Eric Carle in *The Very Hungry Caterpillar*, for instance. This technique can also extend to the combination of many other materials: old photographs, tickets, candy wrappers, magazines, newspapers, brochures, fabrics and found objects – manufactured and natural. Be aware that if you combine papers and flat materials with three-dimensional objects, they cannot be scanned for reproduction and the artwork will have to be photographed.

Experiment with collage. Collect as many varied paper samples as you can: bought, found, hand-treated; photographs, text and images from magazines; and anything else paper-based you can think of. Experiment with cutting and ripping the samples up. Layer and glue them onto a base of thick paper or card to make your composition.

COPYRIGHT

Most artists working in this way have vast collections of all sorts of miscellaneous materials, although you must remember not to infringe on copyright laws if your work is going to be reproduced. It is therefore safer to use your own original photographic imagery within your illustrations.

Layered media
A variety of media combine here to create a rich and atmospheric, densely layered piece.

Coloured pencils

Oil pastels

Gouache paint

Scissors

Tissue paper

READ THIS

The Art of Eric Carle
by Eric Carle (2002)

An autobiography of the artist – an excellent example of paper collage at its best.

Collage Sourcebook
by Jennifer Atkinson (2004)

A good sourcebook for anyone interested in collage techniques. Step-by-step projects and instructions on various techniques.

An Introduction to Mixed Media
by Michael Wright and Ray Smith (1995)

A practical guide to a range of techniques, with gallery pages and step-by-step instructions.

ACRYLIC AND OIL PASTEL

Once you have mastered the basic techniques, there is a whole range of effects that can be achieved by mixing traditional media together. For an illustrator, it is very important to find a distinctive style – similar to a personal signature. A style can be based on drawing technique and special use of media.

1 This example combines acrylic paint used as a background and oil pastel, which is built up over the top. The acrylic is applied with a large flat brush in bold, sketchy strokes. The paint is diluted to allow the paper to show through.

2 When the pastel is laid down and blended, the acrylic wash is still visible underneath. This gives the pastel a textural appearance, very different from a single layer of pastel.

3 The rest of the design is then applied over the acrylic wash, using the same techniques of blending as for traditional oil pastel.

4 The final design is then fixed to prevent any unintended smudging. (Tip: a cheaper alternative to store-bought fixative is hairspray.)

CUT PAPER

This technique is similar to the ancient art of mosaic, which was used in classical Greece and Rome to decorate the floors and walls of villas. It has become a very popular technique for producing decorative illustrations and is often seen on wine labels or food illustrations.

1 The design is drawn out onto the base paper. The other papers are cut to size with a scalpel or scissors and then stuck down.

2 For more difficult areas, the design can be drawn on layout paper and then stuck onto the mosaic paper with small drops of glue. Cut through both layers to obtain accurate shapes.

3 Try to keep the design as simple as possible – cutting tiny details can be very time-consuming and ineffective. The glues most appropriate for this method are the kind that dry clear, so that any residue will not show on the finished work.

TORN PAPER FLOWER COLLAGE

For this collage technique, you may use precoloured papers or paint your own.
First tear the background shapes, then make the patterns and flower petals.
If you are adding a name or greeting, make it at this point and decide where
it will fit. Assemble the flower, then glue all of the component parts in place,
starting with the background and working up.

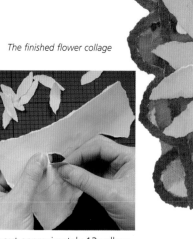

The finished flower collage

1 For the main background, paint a gradated wash of red and orange (mixed from yellow and red). Paint more sheets of paper using yellow, cobalt blue, turquoise blue, lime green and cream.

2 Tear or cut the background rectangles from turquoise, red/orange and lime green papers. Make sure they will all fit onto your folded card and still leave a slight border area.

3 Tear out approximately 13 yellow petals for the flower, making each one similar in size.

4 Tear the wavy cobalt blue border shapes, cream dots and a spiral for the middle of the flower. You can draw the shapes with a pencil first to help make them more accrate, but remember to erase any pencil lines.

5 Glue the end of each flower petal on the back. Assemble the flower by gluing the edge of the petals onto a green central circle. Place each one equidistant from the last.

6 Glue the background rectangles first, followed by the wavy blue borders, white dots and finally the flower.

When white, painted paper is ripped, one edge will show the white paper base, whereas the other will show only the painted, coloured edge. Exploit this effect in your collage.

ADDING COLOUR TO PHOTOCOPIED SKETCHES

This process also works well with old sheet music and your own sketches. To use your own sketch, take a black and white photocopy. Lightly sand the surface to remove the gloss finish, then apply paint.

1 Using a good-quality black-and-white photocopy of your own sketch, lightly sand the surface using fine sandpaper.

2 Mix a watery consistency of paint and start to outline the sketch. Cover an area of the background to make it look as if your subject was drawn on a coloured background.

3 On the finished image, the unpainted edges of the photocopy have been ripped away.

4 You could try painting strange colours over the photocopy to give the whole image a surreal effect.

PAINTING A FREESTYLE PATTERN

A simple way to make a repeat pattern is by painting shapes freestyle. Use the finished pattern as it is, or as individual shapes.

1 Decide on a simple motif and consider the size you want it to be in your finished pattern. Paint your shape at intervals on textured paper.

2 When the paint is dry, rip or cut out the individual shapes.

3 Arrange the shapes on a different colour or type of paper. Apply glue to the back of each, and stick.

4 The finished sample shows how the scale of each shape can be changed easily. The torn or cutout shapes could be used for a background or border.

DEALING WITH SOURCE MATERIAL

You don't just have to cut out and stick the paper and other materials for your collage. Experiment with other ways of putting things together.

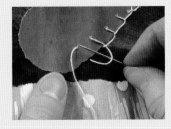

Stitching paper shapes
Carefully stitch shapes together using coloured thread and bold, sculptural embroidery stitches. Use this technique to add accents and emphasis.

Chamfered paper edges
Tear the paper insted of cutting it out to exploit the two-tone and textural effects that result.

Weaving paper
Play with the three-dimensional nature of collage by interweaving paper strips.

DIGITAL

Computers have become a very popular tool for illustrators who want to create colourful and sophisticated images that can be manipulated and amended at the touch of a key. Do remember, though, that a computer is only a tool and can only be as creative and effective as the person using it.

Keep a sketchbook to scan from.

A scanner will scan your linework to allow you to colour or manipulate it digitally.

A graphics tablet allows you to draw more accurately.

SCANNED DRAWINGS

Many computer-generated illustrations are original scanned line drawings. Software is then used to add colour or textures to complete the artwork. A graphics tablet gives you the freedom of a pen and enables you to draw directly onto the screen; many have pressure-sensitive tips for extra control. Software packages offer a wide range of predefined brushes designed to emulate existing media. The range of opportunities within digital illustration can be daunting at first, but after selecting the most appropriate program it is a matter of practice and experimentation. Mistakes are easily rectified with the "undo" command!

This dragon has been drawn by hand and scanned into Photoshop. It has then been cut out from the white background using the magic wand tool, and the image of the head placed on a separate layer (see page 137) so that any colouring or manipulation is confined to the head and does not affect the white background. By altering the levels in the Hue/Saturation (see page 137) the whole head has been shaded pink. The areas that are a different colour were selected using the lasso tool and individually coloured.

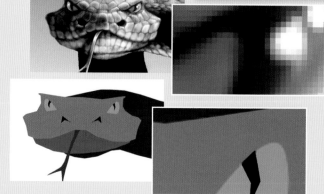

BITMAP OR VECTOR?

An important thing to take into consideration when approaching digital illustration is the difference between bitmap and vector graphics. Software packages such as Photoshop and Paint are programs that use bitmap graphics, in which each pixel on the screen is a coloured block; this creates images which are resolution-dependent and will appear "soft" if they are enlarged too much. Packages such as Illustrator and Flash use vector graphics, in which mathematically calculated curves are used to generate the imagery. These can be enlarged to almost any size.

TRY THIS

The best way to understand and feel confident with the various software is to play with and explore the possibilities, as you would with other media or tools. Take a drawing from your sketchbook and scan it, then have fun manipulating, layering and colouring; wherever your imagination takes you! Try it in Photoshop initially.

WEBSITES

www.paintermagazine.co.uk

www.pshopcreative.co.uk

www.computerarts.co.uk/tutorials

www.lynda.com

Working in layers

Illustrator and Photoshop use layers to build up illustrations, manipulate images and create montages of multiple images. It is very important to master the use and organization of layers. This vector illustration of a teddy has been created in Illustrator; the ability to turn layers on and off shows how you can experiment with the final composition. Layers are useful for collage-type compositions, adding and superimposing images and switching the order of them for different effects.

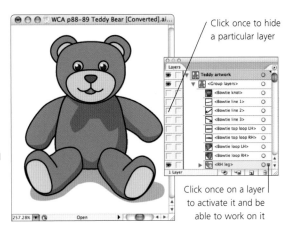

Click once to hide a particular layer

Click once on a layer to activate it and be able to work on it

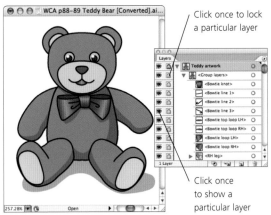

Click once to lock a particular layer

Click once to show a particular layer

Working with effects and filters

Photoshop is used to work creatively with bitmap images. It has a large collection of brushes, filters and effects with which to create interesting results. This montage has been created using seven separate photographs. The pen tool was used to draw paths in order to cut out parts of the photographs and place them onto the main canvas, on separate layers. The magic wand can also be used for this if the background is a plain contrasting colour (such as the fish). Each image can then be manipulated individually before "flattening" the canvas as the final montage.

1 The duck was cut out using the pen tool to make a bezier path. Selecting the path, the duck is copied and pasted onto the main canvas. The flying birds, balloon fish and plane were cut out, copied and pasted in the same way.

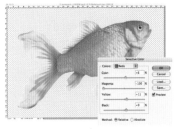

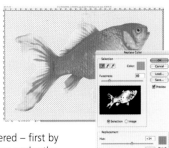

2 The colouring of the fish has been altered – first by using Selective colour, then Replace colour under the Image/adjustment menu.

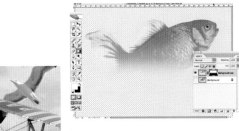

3 A vector mask and the gradient tool created a fade effect to merge the fish into the sea in the final composition. The sea and sky background was merged using the same tools.

4 The sky layer was altered using the Hue/Saturation function under the Image/adjustment menu.

Computer collage

Collage is a particular traditional medium that has benefited from technological developments.

49 MAKING A DUMMY BOOK

A dummy book is a small, three-dimensional model of your picture book. The first one you make will be for your benefit – you'll be surprised at how your perception of the pace, rhythm and sequence of the story changes when you hold a tangible version in your hands. The second will be a full-sized model that you'll show to your publisher.

Safety note: work in a well-ventilated room on a protective surface.

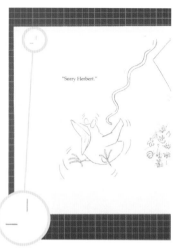

PREPARING PAGES FOR A MOCK-UP BOOK

1 Prepare artwork as line drawings, with text for each of the double page spreads, and add registration marks. (These can be original drawn roughs or scanned and printed.)

2 Trim all double pages along registration marks to printed page size.

3 Arrange all the pages in order, from the front endpaper to the back endpaper.

4 Fold each trimmed double page in half.

5 Flatten the folded edge using a bone folder (or similar tool).

6 Stack all the pages together. Check that they are even and level by tapping them on a flat surface at 90 degrees.

MAKING UP THE BOOK

1 Take the first double page, which will be the front endpaper.

2 Place a clean piece of scrap paper in the fold.

3 Spray the back of the page with spray mount.

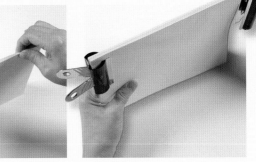

4 Line up the second double page along the spine. Place it onto the sprayed page and smooth it down to secure it.

5 Repeat this process until all the pages are stuck together.

6 Press down the pages along the spine, to make sure they are all securely glued and even.

7 Place bulldog clips on each end to hold the papers securely.

8 Brush PVA glue along the spine.

9 Attach a strip of thin paper, the width of the spine, along the glued spine.

10 Press down firmly. Leave the book to dry completely for at least a few hours, or preferably overnight.

MAKING THE COVER USING BOOK CLOTH

1 Cut out two pieces of cover board, 2–5 mm (⅛–¼ in) larger on three sides than your glued book, and a strip of board the same width as the spine and the same height as the cover board.

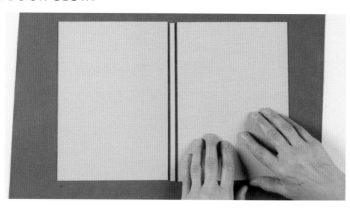

2 Place the two cover boards and the spine onto a piece of book cloth with a 2–5 mm (⅛–¼ in) gap between the spine and covers. Cut the book cloth at least 25 mm (1 in) larger all around. Spray-mount or glue (PVA) the pieces of cover board to the cloth.

3 Turn over and smooth down the book cloth to get rid of any air bubbles, and press along the edges.

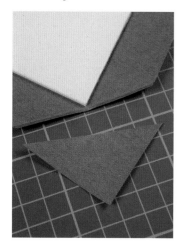

6 Trim the book cloth at the corners about 2 mm (⅛ in) away from the crease.

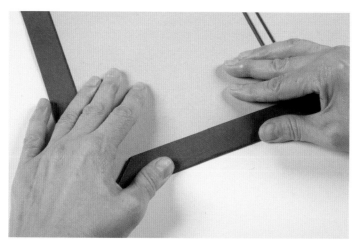

7 Fold each of the edges of the book cloth onto each of the cover board edges and crease firmly.

8 Use a brush to dab small amounts of PVA glue (or a glue stick) onto each length, starting with the top and bottom of the cover.

4 Trim the book cloth evenly around the glued cover boards, no smaller than 20 mm (⅝ in) all around.

5 Fold the book cloth over each corner of the cover and make a crease.

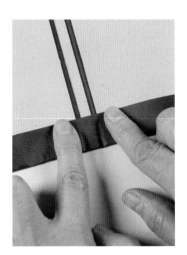

9 Press down well, working from the centre out.

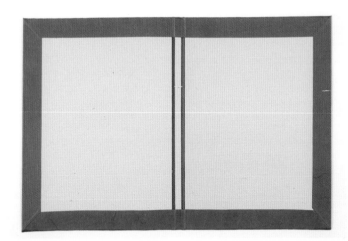

10 When all the edges are glued, they should meet neatly at the corners. Leave the glued cover to dry for a few hours.

11 Fold the cover and start to manipulate the spine with your hands, so that it is flexible and the back and front covers can move freely.

PUTTING THE BOOK AND THE COVER TOGETHER

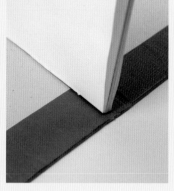

1 Place a clean piece of scrap paper between the first endpaper and the rest of the book.

2 Spray the back of the page with spray mount.

3 Position the book along the edge of the front cover board.

4 Make sure that the space on each side of the cover is equal.

THE DUST JACKET

1 Prepare artwork in the same way as for covering a book. Trim the height of the scanned or photocopied artwork along the registration marks to fit the height of the cover of the book.

2 Measure the width of the spine.

3 Mark the measurement on the cover illustration.

4 Fold and press down using the bone folder to create the spine width.

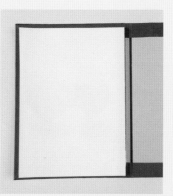

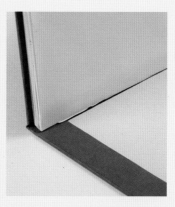

5 Bring the glued endpaper down onto the cover and press down firmly.

6 Place a clean piece of scrap paper between the back endpaper and the rest of the book. Make sure that the back cover board is also covered.

7 Spray the back of the endpaper with spray mount. Line the book along the edge of the back cover board and press the glued page down. Close the book.

8 Press the spine and cover so it creases the spine and book covers. The process works with both an illustrated piece of paper and plain book cloth for the cover.

5 Place the book into the folded space and fold the ends of the dust jacket around the ends of the book to create back and front flaps.

6 Fold down firmly using the bone folder to complete the book and dust jacket.

TOP TIP

When you design and illustrate the cover, allow for the extra measurements of the cover boards, spine, gaps in between and the amount that will fold over the edges of the cover board.

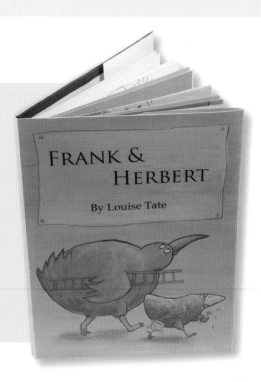

FRANK & HERBERT

By Louise Tate

Acting like a professional
Act like a professional and you won't get eaten for breakfast. This chapter gives you some guidelines.

Chapter six

PROFESSIONAL PRACTICE

There are plenty of things first-time authors or illustrators can do to help themselves in their quest for a publisher. This section shows you some approaches to adopt.

50 WORKING LIFE

Being able to commit time and space to your work is an important factor in how successfully you will be able to develop your career.

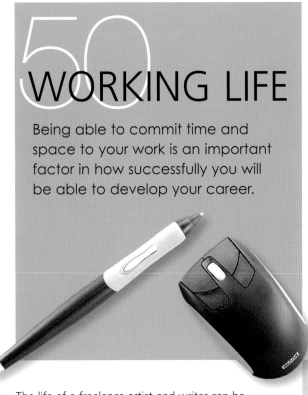

Having somewhere to work in your home allows you to make the most of your time. A spare room is ideal, but essentially all you need is a designated workspace with room for computer equipment and a telephone. Decide how much space you actually need and be ingenious in creating a place you can leave undisturbed – a workstation under the stairs or in the attic are two obvious examples.

Working in a studio with other artists can be inspiring and fun and allows you to share the running costs. But it can also be disruptive and expensive, with the rent and the commute to a studio a factor in your monthly outgoings. There are advantages to being able to pool resources, share contacts and publicize yourself as a group. If you take this route, make sure you find like-minded people to share a space with.

Be organized
Have everything close at hand in your workstation. You don't want to have to scramble around looking for a brush or photo reference.

The life of a freelance artist and writer can be immensely rewarding. Being in control of your working day is a major plus. Working on something creative that you love doing and that will hopefully enrich children's lives is also fantastic. However, the life of a freelancer working from home can also be an isolating experience, with much of your contact with others conducted via email and telephone. It can be insecure financially, too. Few writers or illustrators are lucky enough to have a steady stream of work.

Maximize space
If space is at a premium, consider keeping all of your equipment in a portable container, such as an art box, that can be moved around easily.

Work checklist

If you want to become a writer or illustrator, think about the following issues:

- How much time can you commit to the enterprise? Is it going to be a full-time, all-or-nothing endeavour, or is it part of an equation that also includes childcare and part-time work?

- How much space do you need to work? Illustrators traditionally work on quite a small scale, but increasingly this does not have to be the case. You will need space to store artwork as well as a place to generate it from.

- Do you want to work in isolation or would you prefer to share a workspace with others?

- Do you want to engage the services of an agent or are you happier promoting yourself?

- Do you need to engage the services of an accountant or are you confident that you can manage your finances on your own?

Each of these questions needs careful consideration as there is no right or wrong way to approach freelancing – only the way that is best for you.

BUSINESS ESSENTIALS

Invest in some well printed stationery with your own letterhead and logo design to use for correspondence. A business card and compliment slips are also very useful. You will need to generate an invoice template if you have a computer, or use a duplicate book from a stationery store if you don't.

Invoices should include a unique number (devise your own system), your name and contact details, the name and company of the person who commissioned you, a description of the job and the agreed fee for the work completed. Keep a copy of each invoice you send out and make a note when it has been paid.

It's official! A purchase order from the publisher (below) confirms your commission. You will be expected to sign and return it, along with an invoice (right) for work completed. Don't forget to include your name and address, or they won't know where to send the cheque.

LIZ DALBY
liz-dalby@hotmail.co.uk
07876 230333

Writing, illustration
and editorial services

If you're an illustrator, design your own stationery, and use it as an opportunity to showcase your skills.

INVOICE

Dean Bassinger
4488 Mandy Way
Hill Valley CA 94941
Tel: 415-384-5368
email: deabs@yahoo.com

To: Patricia Whyte
Art Director
Finest Book Publishing
909 Liondale
Philadelphia
PA 400321

Date: June 20, 2004

Order number: 028-04
Reference code: ICB

To supply: 3 full color illustrations
6 black and white line drawings

(@ 300dpi on disc)

Total: $500

FINEST
Book Publishing

PURCHASE ORDER FOR CREATIVE WORK

THIS PURCHASE ORDER DOES NOT ACT AS AN INVOICE.

PLEASE INVOICE WHEN THE WORK IS COMPLETED

TO: DATE:

PROJECT TITLE: BOOK CODE:

RETURN TO:

DESCRIPTION OF WORK:

DELIVER BY:
(Failure to deliver the work on time or in accordance with the above brief may result in a reduction in or cancellation of the agreed fee.)

AGREED FEE:

In consideration of the abovementioned fee paid by Finest Book Publishing to me on delivery and acceptance of the work described above, I hereby grant to Finest Book Publishing ownership of the a non-exclusive license in the said work for the full period of copyright and all renewals and extensions Finest Book Publishing agrees to credit me as the originator of the work. I warrant that the work is original, has not previously been published in any form except as disclosed by me above and is in no way a violation or an infringement of any existing copyright or licence. I hereby indemnify Finest Book Publishing against all actions, suits, proceedings, claims, demands, damages and costs occasioned to Finest Book Publishing in consequence of any breach of this warranty or arising from any claim

SIGNATURE OF CONTRIBUTOR: DATE:

SIGNED FOR AND ON BEHALF OF
FINEST BOOK PUBLISHING BY: DATE:

Please sign and return the green copy of this form to Finest Book Publishing with your invoice. Keep the pink copy as your reference.

FINEST BOOK PUBLISHING   909 LIONDALE   PHILADELPHIA   PA 400321
TEL (215) 770-0670   FAX (215) 770-0671

ACQUIRING AN AGENT

An agent can be extremely useful and will promote your work in an effective and professional manner. He or she will negotiate the appropriate fee for your work, and field requests from clients. Agents take around 15 per cent of any money earned through them. Once you work with an agent it is considered bad form to take on work directly.

Agents are interested in seeing new talent, but do not always have the time for a personal appointment. Approach them by sending a letter and samples of your work through the mail. If you have a website, direct them to this, too. All files you send should be compatible with PC and Mac computers. After sending your work, follow up with a phone call to check that it's arrived, but don't bombard agents with calls or correspondence.

READ THIS

The Children's Writers' and Artists' Yearbook

An invaluable resource, updated annually, listing contact details of agents and publishers in the US, UK,

Equipment you will need:

Essential:

- Studio equipment
- A desk and a comfortable chair with back support
- A desk-lamp with a daylight simulation bulb (to ensure your colors stay true even when you're working at night)
- A telephone and answering machine (landline or mobile)
- A plan chest for storing your artwork safely
- A filing system for correspondence

For the longer term:

- A computer for graphics software and email
- A scanner for sending roughs
- A color printer for printing samples
- A graphics tablet

51 COPYRIGHT AND LICENSING

As the originator of artwork, you automatically own the copyright to any imagery you produce, whether it is a doodle you did while you were on the phone or a fully realized painting.

WHAT IS COPYRIGHT?

Copyright means the right to copy something, hence the name. You automatically own the copyright to your artwork, but it is possible to sell or gift this right to someone else. Copyright does not necessarily reside in the physical object, but in the right for it to be copied. Someone can own the copyright to your painting without owning the original.

Traditional copyright would give you sole right to approve any copied versions of your artwork, and will not enter the public domain until 70 years after your death. What this means is that it becomes common property, and although you would still be attributed as the creator, the right to copy it is now free to all.

Copyright can be bequeathed, and in some cases extended. For example, the copyright for the story of *Peter Pan* was given to Great Ormond Street Children's Hospital in London, and continues to generate revenue for them.

Don't skim the contract
Always clarify with the publisher what rights you are assigning them – whether they can reproduce your work once or continually, and how you will be compensated for it.

READ THIS

Illustrator's Guide to Law and Business Practice
by Simon Stern (2008)

This is an extremely useful and practical guide that explains in detail all aspects of law that an illustrator should be familiar with, including terms and conditions, calculating fees and license agreements.

The Future of Ideas
by Lawrence Lessig (2002)

If you are interested in the idea of copyright and the legal implications of intellectual ownership in an increasingly piratical digital age, then you may enjoy reading about the creative commons movement.

http://lessig.org/blog

Option clauses
Some contracts include a clause that keeps you from selling the work to other publishers, or states the course of action if the publisher should go out of business or the book goes out of print. If you're uncertain about the terms, seek legal advice.

COPYRIGHT IN CRISIS

Copyright law is currently in crisis due to the ease of duplicating imagery digitally. Organizations such as "Creative Commons" argue the case for a more flexible approach to copyright. However, as a professional artist, it is imperative that you protect your right to be identified and recompensed as the originator of the artwork. The best way to do this is to always insist on retaining copyright of your artwork, but agree to license the work for the specific use intended by your client.

LICENSING

A license allows the client clearly defined rights to use the imagery in a specified format for a specified amount of time and in specified places. Licenses are frequently used for developing a character, as a successful children's book character can generate spin-off merchandise in everything from bedding and toys to food and clothes. It would be very disappointing for you if you realized you had sold your copyright on a creation that became a runaway global success!

Licenses are used to clarify the use of imagery where the following issues may arise:

- **Use:** this is usually clear from the brief, but it may be worth stating that further uses will require a further fee.

- **Area:** the usual categories for this are UK, Europe, USA and World. The fee should reflect how widely your image is to be distributed.

- **Exclusivity:** the client will want to be clear that they have the exclusive right to use the image. This covers all areas of reproduction for example not only the book but stationery, greetings cards, t-shirts to film and digital rights – in some circumstances you might be able to keep an aspect of this to help boost your fee.

- **Duration:** this is often not clear, and the solution is to give a very long license, even for the duration of copyright.

- **Royalties:** a publisher will offer you a contract that states the terms of the advance and the royalties. The royalties are the percentage of the profits made after the advance is paid back.

CONTRACTS

It is vitally important that you are clear about the use of your artwork, and you should always be aware of what you are being contracted to do. A contract can be a written or verbal agreement, but if it is verbal it is best to follow up the conversation with a letter or email clarifying that both sides understand the terms and conditions of what you are expected to do, and where this obligation ends. Otherwise you may find yourself endlessly tinkering with artwork that should have been approved at an earlier stage.

Protecting your copyright

The simplest way to ensure protection of your copyright is to place a copy of your artwork in a sealed envelope and post it to yourself. Do not open the envelope when it arrives, but keep it safe! This document could be used in a court of law to prove your prior claim to the imagery if any misappropriation of your work occurs.

Who owns what?

One day you may create a character who has licensing potential. You'll want to be sure that you own the rights you thought you owned.

52 SHOWING YOUR WORK

Your "book", or portfolio, is the public face of your work. It should show off your capabilities and ideas in a variety of styles and media while maintaining coherency and consistency. It should also contain a concise resumé detailing your skills. You may consider compiling different portfolios for different markets. Some children's illustrators even work under different names (or pseudonyms) if they have several styles of working.

THE IDEAL PORTFOLIO

The ideal children's book illustration portfolio would contain:

- drawings that are full of life and personality
- character studies showing a character in many moods and poses
- evidence of good composition and visual storytelling skills
- black-and-white work as well as full-colour
- good use of media

Don't put half-finished work in. Show off your skills! If you don't have ideas for your own stories, it is a good idea to include some illustrations from a well-known fairy tale in your portfolio, as this will give an art director a clear idea of how you approach interpreting a text.

MEETING THE ART DIRECTOR

You have your bright and shiny portfolio with your work displayed coherently and cleanly within. You have printed some business cards to leave as a reminder of you and your work after you have gone. If you are used to working alone at home, you may want to assess your habitual work clothes when setting off to a meeting. This is a rare occasion on which you must look presentable! You are about to meet with someone who is interested in your work.

- Make eye contact, smile and shake hands. Research has shown that people make up their minds about potential employees within a couple of seconds of meeting them. As so much of children's publishing is based on collaboration, it is important that you come across as friendly and enthusiastic.

- Be confident about your work when talking an art director through your folder – there is no need to point out what you don't like about an image. Highlight your strengths.

- Don't explain everything in enormous detail. The art director is busy and needs to get a quick sense of what your work is like, not a history of every job you have ever done.

TRY THIS

Invest in a professional portfolio with clear sleeves. Think about the size – it doesn't have to be huge, but neither should it be minuscule. Consider what you want to achieve. Do you want to show a lot of double-page spreads from books you are working on? How big are the originals? Have your work copied to a high standard, and include original pieces, too. The portfolio should be clear and clean (no dust, hairs, or footprints!) and should be ordered in a logical way – nobody wants to have to root through piles of paper to get a sense of your work. Around 20 pieces should be ample to give someone a sense of your range and skills. Mount your work securely in the sleeves using double-sided tape.

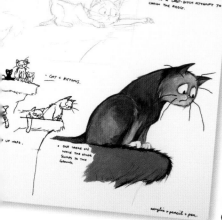

Unfinished work
Avoid the impulse to put unfinished
work in your portfolio.

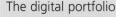

MARKETING YOUR WORK

There are many ways in which you can attract the attention of a commissioning editor or art buyer. Word of mouth through contacts and friends is the most direct and low-key way to start. Or, exhibit your work in local and national galleries and enter competitions. Direct mailshots of your own promotional pack are a good way to show your work around. Another option is to buy space in one of the illustration annuals such as *American Illustration*. These are sent out to thousands of potential clients and – although expensive – can pay for themselves in terms of the amount of work they generate. You need to balance the advantages of targeting people you have researched very specifically against the advantages of the "scattergun" approach. The first is time-consuming; the second expensive. But both can work equally well.

MORE ONLINE OPTIONS

Another option is to sign up to a group website. These have the advantage of being low-maintenance, but they are often vast and the danger is your work will become lost or swamped by the sheer volume of imagery on display. They are also not free, although the cost is small compared to creating and maintaining your own site. The Association of Illustrators has a reputable online portfolio site based around the 'Images' book it publishes every year showcasing the best of British Illustration. (http://www.aoiportfolios.com/)

A "blog" can be an effective way to keep your work in the public eye. They are often free and allow you to upload images and text very easily into a limited set of formats. The content is easily managed and can be updated as often as you like. Many artists choose this form because it allows them to show new work easily, and as it is constantly being updated there is more chance of people returning for a second, third or even daily look! The blog allows you to index your work into categories and will archive your entries. Blogs may be simper than a flash-based website, but they are functional, easy and can be run alongside a more traditional portfolio-based website.

The digital portfolio

Having a website is a definite advantage for an illustrator, as it is an easy way to direct people to look at your work. However, not all art directors like to spend their time sifting through the enormous variety of work online, or waiting for large files to download. You will not automatically get the attention you expect from sending out work in this format. You will still need to use traditional methods to attract some potential commissioners. It is also not enough to build a beautiful website and expect people to find it by chance.

The advantage of having a digital or online portfolio is that it allows you to show time-based work, animated pieces of work and work with sound files attached. Not all of children's publishing is paper-based, and increasingly children will access content online. This is a tremendously exciting area for illustrators to be aware of, and if you are interested in the possibilities of digital interaction and animation in your ideas for children's publishing, then now is the ideal time for you! Remember, your work does not necessarily have to be generated by a computer to be displayed by one; often traditional work reproduces extraordinarily well on-screen.

READ THIS

GOOD EXAMPLES OF ARTISTS' WEBSITES/BLOGS:

- **Bridget Strevens**
  http://bridgetstrevens.com

- **Joel Stewart**
  http://joel-stewart.
  blogspot.com/

53

GETTING A COMMISSION

Congratulations! Your work has made an impression and an art director has asked you to produce some work for them. Do not be afraid of asking straightforward questions if you are not clear about what the task is that you are being asked to do.

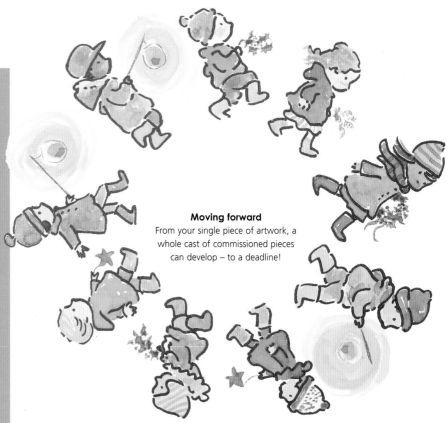

Moving forward
From your single piece of artwork, a whole cast of commissioned pieces can develop – to a deadline!

A clear vision
Make sure you know what the brief is before you start writing, illustrating or even sketching out ideas.

Useful questions

The following questions may help you clarify with the publisher or art director the particular task in front of you:

- What exactly are you being asked to do? Avoid producing speculative artwork for nothing. However, you can discuss developing ideas and roughs if you are offered a development fee.

- What is the outcome of the work? Is it to be a book? If so, ask about the format and extent of the book.

- When is the deadline? Is the deadline realistic? If not, say so. You know better than anyone how long a piece of artwork is going to take you to do.

- Where is the book being published? A picture book may be translated into many different languages. This may impact the kind of details you can put

into the imagery – for example, yellow taxis and red postboxes are specific to particular places.

- How is the work to be presented? Are you expected to send the originals or will a high-resolution scan be fine?

- How much are you going to get paid? Although illustrators are notoriously shy of talking about money, it does you no favours to let yourself to be exploited. Your work has commercial value, and you must appreciate your time.

- Ask how any advance payments would be structured. Ask about royalties.

Negotiation

Tips for negotiating a good deal:

- Be confident when talking about money, without sounding arrogant or demanding. You can be polite and pleased that you have been commissioned without being astonished and overly grateful!

- Be clear about what you can do and what you expect from the publisher. State at the beginning that you expect to retain copyright on your imagery.

- Be mindful of the client's needs as well as your own.

- Be pleasant and cooperative – strive to be polite and professional at all times.

- Be prepared to pass up the job if the terms are not acceptable to you.

ROYALTIES

Royalty agreements usually form the basis of the transaction between the publisher and the author or illustrator. A publisher agrees to invest in the expertise and knowledge of the writer or illustrator by advancing them money to enable them to produce the work. The publisher offers the contributor a percentage of the ongoing profits of their joint enterprise once this initial advance has been repaid. Therefore a large advance means that it takes longer for a book to start earning royalties for you. But if your book is successful, the royalty payments will continue to come in for many years after your initial effort.

Royalties in picture books are usually split 50/50 between the writer and the illustrator. Sometimes this seems unfair, as the text may be minimal yet the illustrations are lavish and detailed. In this case it would be up to you as the illustrator (or your agent) to negotiate a bigger percentage of the royalties.

BOOK PACKAGING

Book packaging differs from publishing in the following important respects. Packagers do not store, distribute or market the books they produce. They concentrate on creating the book, and then sell it on to a publishing house as an edition or co-edition. Packagers are, in essence, a "freelance" editorial/design/ production unit. They can vary from being very small outfits to larger companies, and in general offer less generous advances than the publishing houses.

Going to print
Remember that the illustrations you supply to a publisher are going out to the world and will be in print for many years to come. This is your moment to shine.

The real deal
A skilful negotiator will get the best deal for the characters they have created.

GLOSSARY

A beginner's guide to print and publishing terminology

BLAD A booklet used in book publishing and usually made up of the intended cover and three to eight printed sample pages. Used to promote new titles at book fairs, sales conferences and so on.

Bleed (1) Printed matter designed to run off the edge of the paper. Also used by bookbinders to describe over-cut margins. (2) An ink that changes colour or mixes with other colours, sometimes caused by lamination.

Blow-up An enlargement from a small original.

Blurb Promotional text on the flap of a book jacket or the outside back cover of a paperback. Often the listed merits on the back of a book are called "bullets".

Body type Text normally used for the main text of a book, not captions or headings. The size range is usually 6 to 16 point. Picture books may have a body type size up to 30 point.

Bulk The thickness of paper – spine widths are calculated from paper bulk and number of pages.

Combination line and halftone work Halftone and line work combined on one set of films, plates or artwork.

Continuous tone Illustration (photograph, drawing or painting) consisting of a broad range of tone.

Copy Manuscript, typescript, transparency or artwork from which a printed image is to be prepared. May also be supplied in electronic form.

Copyright The right of an author or artist to control the use of their original work. Although broadly controlled by international agreement there are substantial differences between countries.

Corner marks These may be on the original artwork, film or printed sheet and can also serve as register marks during printing or as cut marks for use in the finishing operations.

Cropping Trimming or masking a photograph or artwork so that a detail, its proportions or size are in line with those required.

Cut marks Marks printed on a sheet to indicate the edge of a page to be trimmed.

Cut-out (1) An illustration from which the background has been removed to provide a silhouette. (2) A display card or book cover with a pattern die-cut in it.

Die-cut Steel cutting rules bent into an image shape and used to cut into board or paper – used in novelty books.

Display type Any type other than body copy designed to catch attention, for examples, heads and titles, often unusual, highly decorative or distorted faces in size 16 to 72 point.

Double-page spread *See spread.*

Dummy A sample for a job made up with the actual materials and to the correct size to show bulk, style of binding and so on. Also a complete mock-up of a job showing position of type matter and illustrations, margins and other details.

Endpapers Lining sheets used at each end of a book to fasten the case to the first and last sections of a case binding.

Etching The mordant effect of a chemical on plate or film. In lithography, the solutions are applied to the plate after imaging to make the non-image sections both water-attractive and ink-repellent.

Flat colour An area of printed colour with no tonal variations.

Flush left or right Type set to line up at the left or right of a column.

Folio (1) A page number and also a page. (2) A large book in which the full-size sheet only needs to be folded once before binding.

Font A set of type of one face or size.

Format The shape and size of a book (and sometimes the binding style and overall layout of the page).

Four-colour process Colour printing by means of the three primary colours (yellow, magenta, cyan) and black superimposed. Each plate is produced from separations which have been made from the originals on a scanner or process camera.

Grain The direction in which the fibres lie in a piece of paper – some strongly-textured papers can add interesting effects in washes and shadows to watercolour paintings.

Graphics tablet Used in computing by compositors and in electronic-page composition systems for layout or system control.

Gutter The margin down the centre of a double-page spread, sometimes equal to to two back margins.

Half up Instruction to prepare artwork 50 per cent larger than final size so that it can be reproduced at 66 per cent to eliminate any blemishes in the original.

Halftone Printing tone illustrations by breaking them down photographically into dots – used in lithography.

Imposition Plan for placing pages on a printing sheet so that when folded, each page will be in the correct sequence.

In proportion (1) Individual items of artwork that are to be enlarged or reduced by the same amount during reproduction. (2) Instruction that one dimension of an artwork is to be enlarged/reduced in the same proportion as the other.

ISBN International Standard Book Number. A unique ten-figure number that identifies the language of publication of a book, its publisher and its title, plus a check digit. Often also included in a barcode.

Justify Positioning of type lines so they are evenly spaced on left and right.

Laminating Applying transparent or coloured plastic films, usually with a high gloss finish, to printed matter to protect or enhance it. Various films are available with different gloss, folding and strength characteristics.

Line art Artwork entirely in black on white with no intermediary tones.

Layout Any indication for the organization of text and pictures with instructions about sizing and so on for reproduction or printing.

Lightbox A box with a translucent glass top lit from below giving a balanced light suitable for colour matching on which colour transparencies, prints, and proofs can be examined or compared.

Monochrome A single colour.

Mordant (1) Adhesive for fixing gold leaf. (2) Fluid used to etch lines on a printing plate.

Offset (1) Lithographic (and sometimes letterpress) method of printing in which the ink is transferred from the printing plate to an offset blanket cylinder, and then to the paper, board, metal, or whatever on which it is required. (2) To reproduce a book in one edition by photographing a previously printed edition.

Prelims Pages at the beginning of a book consisting of half-title, title page, copyright page, contents and other pre-text materials such as acknowledgements and introduction.

Proof A representation on paper of any type or other image made either from the plates or directly from the film used in their production.

Recto Right-hand page.

Reproduction The entire printing process from the completion of typesetting until litho plates reach the press. This includes the use of process cameras, scanners, retouching and the imposition and plate-making operation.

Rough An unfinished layout or design.

Rough proof A proof that is not necessarily in position or on the correct paper.

Section Paper folded to form part of a book or booklet. Sections can be made up of sheets folded to 4, 8, 16 but rarely more than 128 pages, perhaps from two 64-page sections.

Spread Printed matter spread across two facing pages.

Vignette Effect applied to halftones that, instead of being squared up or cut out, have the tone etched gently away at the edges.

Verso Left-hand page.

INDEX

CREDITS

Quarto would like to thank the following artists and agencies for kindly supplying images for inclusion in this book:

- **Brian Fijimori**
  www.dasgroup.com 6tr

- **Annebicque Bernard** ©/Corbis 74t

- **Dover publications** 10b, 11br

- *Farmer Duck* by Martin Waddell and illustrated by Helen Oxenbury. Reproduced by permission of Walker Books Ltd, London SE11 5HJ. Illustrations © 1991 Helen Oxenbury 32

- *Ginger* by Charlotte Voake. Reproduced by permission of Walker Books Ltd, London SE11 5HJ. Illustrations © 1997 Charlotte Voake 16b

- *Harry Potter* by J K Rowling, children's jacket illustrated by Cliff Wright (tl), adults jacket illustrated by Michael Wildsmith (tr) and published by Bloomsbury 72

- *Marvin Wanted More* by Joseph Theobald and published by Bloomsbury 130tr

- **Nicole Tadgell illustrations** © Nicole Tadgell nic.art@verizon.net 1, 10tr, 26tr, 27t, 45tr, 51ml, 52m, 81m, 84-85, 105

- *Pudding* by Pippa Godhart, illustrated by Caroline Jayne Church. Published by Rachel Ortas 44tr

- **Shutterstock** 15b, 18m&b, 20tr, 21bl, 49tl, 59, 60bl, 61, 62-69, 78, 106bl, 107tr, 110tr

- **Simon Bartram**, from *Man on the Moon – A Day in the Life of Bob* published by Templar Publishing www.templarco.co.uk

- **Stacey Schuett** www. staceyschuett.com 51tl, 51br, 81tl, 91bl, 103tr

- *This Little Chick* by John Lawrence. Produced by permission of Walker Books Ltd, London SE11 5HJ. Illustrations © 2002 John Lawrence 79b

- *Trolls on Hols* by Alan MacDonald, illustrated by Mark Beech and published by Bloomsbury 56

- *We Are Going On A Bear Hunt* by Michael Rosen and illustrated by Helen Oxenbury. Reproduced by permission of Walker Books Ltd, London SE11 5HJ. Illustrations © 1989 Helen Oxenbury 37b

- *Vegetable Glue* by Susan Chandler © 2004, Illustrated by Elena Odriozola © 2004. Published by Meadowside Children's Books in 2004 13bl&r

- **Jess Wilson** www.jesswilson.co.uk 149

About the contributing authors:

- **Desdemona McCannon** is the award leader for the MA Illustration for Children at North Wales School of Art.

- **Sue Thornton** is an illustrator and senior lecturer at the North Wales School of Art and Design. She has worked as an illustrator for children's books, and is the originator and leader of the BA (Hons) Illustration for Children's Publishing program.

- **Yadzia Williams** is a program leader for BA (Hons) Design: Illustration at the North Wales School of Art and Design at the North East Wales Institute.

- **Paul Dowswell** is a freelance writer, specializing in fiction and non-fiction for children.

- **Meredith Sue Willis**'s books for children include a book about writing, *Blazing Pencils*, and the novels *The Secret Super Powers of Marco*, *Marco's Monster*, and *Billie of Fish House Lane*.

- **Karen Ball** has edited children's non-fiction and fiction for 16 years. She is the author of several children's books and short stories and is currently working on a project set in 13th-century Japan.

We would also like to thank the following artists:

Adam Paxman
Amber Lloyd
Celia Clark
Dai Owen
Daisy Rae
David Bignall
Diane Evans
Emilia Robledo
Gemma Raynor

Heather Allen
Helen Bate
Helen Papworth
Helen Shoesmith
Ian Benfold Haywood
Karina Durrant
Kate Leake
Kathryn Demiss
Katie Cleminson

Kirsteen Harris-Jones
Lee Sullivan
Louise Tate
Lucy Richards
Milena Michalowska
Nadia Sarell
Olga Solabaurieta
Phill O'Connor